The Professional
WORRIER

BECOME THE BOSS
OF YOUR ANXIETY

STEWART GEDDES MIACP

HACHETTE
BOOKS
IRELAND

First published in Ireland in 2019 by HACHETTE BOOKS IRELAND
First published in paperback 2019

Illustration. .... y George
Leonard, copy... tton, an
imprint of Pe.. se LLC.
All rights r... istic, Inc.

Cataloguing in Publication Data is available from the British Library
ISBN 978 1 4736 9032 5
Typeset in Decour by redrattledesign.com
Printed and bound in Great Britain by Clays Ltd, Elcograf S.p.A.

Hachette Books Ireland
8 Castlecourt Centre, Castleknock
Dublin 15, Ireland

A division of Hachette UK Ltd
Carmelite House,
50 Victoria Embankment, EC4Y 0DZ

www.hachettebooksireland.ie

Contents

Chapter 1
No Such Thing as 'Normal'

I have studied anxiety for the past ten years, but I have lived with it for the past forty.

I was a shy kid who grew into a socially anxious teenager. Without exception, when I was faced with fears, I shrank away and sought comfort. To those who knew me, I always seemed happy. As with all human beings, though, there was a lot more happening for me under the surface than I allowed others to see. I was a chronic worrier with inadequate coping skills and a very poor self-image, and I would dip in and out of low mood and an inexplicable sadness from time to time without warning. It took a long time - as I didn't have the tools and insights I now have - but, gradually, I began to understand myself better and get a handle on my emotions and what was really going on for me. I have had to make my peace with what I once saw as the years I lost to anxiety, as if I was to dwell too long on my twenties, it would consume me. I still wish, however, that I could talk to that lost young man, because I know now that anxiety need not have been his master.

I've now figured out what works for me, and this, along with studying some of the great names in the field and working for the past six years with clients struggling with their own anxiety, has given me an understanding about what strategies and approaches can be effective for a lot of people when it comes to managing their mental health. This is what I will talk about in the coming pages.

Everyone is different, and everyone's anxiety plays out in very diverse ways. As a therapist, the last thing I want to do is to presume I know someone else's story or what they need just because I see parallels with my own experiences – but there are many broad similarities in the process that I can use.

So many of the people who come to see me do not know why they feel the way they do, but they know they want something to change. If we struggle with anxiety, we need to become more aware of what is going on for us, we need to gain knowledge about how our minds and bodies work, and have at our disposal some key practical tools to deal with our thoughts, push through fears and accept that this is probably something we will always have to keep on top of going forward. Using elements of Cognitive Behavioural Therapy (CBT), Acceptance and Commitment Therapy (ACT) and some mindfulness techniques, coupled with an understanding of how anxiety works, we can begin to see our minds and bodies as allies and not enemies. They are not looking to harm us, but to protect us. We just need to learn how to work with them, so that they can help us rather than hold us back.

The Professional Worrier is for those who struggle with worry and anxiety to such a degree that it interferes with relationships, studies, careers or a general ability to feel contentment when things appear to be going well. However, this book is not a replacement for therapy, or a comprehensive manual for those who are dealing with Generalised Anxiety Disorder (GAD) or Social Anxiety Disorder.

This book provides an insight into how anxiety and worry work, and how they play out in our social situations, careers and close relationships. It also outlines some practical tips, techniques and strategies to help you manage these issues and situations. I have seen many people – including clients coming through my practice – who just lacked some relevant knowledge and the coping mechanisms to make life so much easier for themselves.

What is 'normal' anyway?

Before we begin, I think it's important to get some widely held misconceptions out of the way, as these can hold us back in any type of personal development work.

The first of these is that, when it comes to how we experience and interact with the rest of the world, and indeed with ourselves, there is such thing as 'normal'.

Before I sought help to tackle my own anxiety, I held an all too common belief that I was somehow different to other people, both those I knew well and those I encountered in the world in general. Because I didn't have access to other people's minds, I believed that my thoughts were very different to theirs; that my thinking was bizarre or odd or in some way 'not normal'. I assumed that my tendency towards negativity, my worrisome thoughts and constant mental noise were things others didn't have to contend with. Other people were normal – I was not.

In my work as a therapist, 'normal' is a theme that comes up again and again for my clients. Nobody is ever able to put their finger on exactly what normal looks like or how it is acted out, but they sure as hell know that they aren't it.

Even though what constitutes normal is never actually fleshed out, and we don't know exactly what it is, we somehow know we don't match up.

This sense of being in some way different and so less acceptable has an effect on us. We cannot believe something about ourselves as fundamental as this and not act from it. If we believe that the world is stacked against us, that everybody else fits in or has things more easy or can get along better, we may feel that we will always be on the outside looking in.

» Is it normal to worry all the time?

» Is it normal to find social interactions difficult?

» Is it normal not to know why we are feeling the way we are feeling?

» Is it normal to find relationships difficult or to be afraid of conflict or to seek comfort when we are feeling anxious?

If we are prone to negative thinking, then 'normal' is probably made up of all the qualities that we do not possess - or, more likely, that we believe we do not possess. Because we have access to our own heads, we know some of the crazy things we think. We know the things we've done that we're not proud of, the hurt we have caused the people we love and the things we do on a daily basis that we wish we didn't.

What we don't have is anyone else's story or all the facts. We may see those around us looking normal, sounding normal, doing the normal things that normal people do. But we don't have access to their dark thoughts, their secrets, their troubled relationships or all the oddities that lie beneath the surface. The human experience is so complex that to be struggling or happy or anxious or sad or in pain or content or lost or overwhelmed or feeling not good enough is all part of the mix. Sometimes, things are going well; sometimes, we feel we can't cope. Each phase comes and goes in a constantly changing cycle.

We may not be perfect beings, but neither is anyone else. Everyone has to contend with pain and suffering. Everyone struggles with uncertainty to some degree. Throw in a mind that can feel like it is working against you, even in good times, and it is hard to imagine what a standard version of normal might look like.

A key part of the work set out in this book, and indeed

in any work we do on our mental health, is that we need to give ourselves a break – to be kinder to ourselves. So, before embarking on this journey, can we at least do this? Can we stop presuming that we are the only person with crazy thoughts, the only one who struggles socially, the only person who worries about the smallest things? Can we try to get to a place where we can begin to see ourselves as good enough? We are a continual work in progress, of course, but we are good enough for the moment and that's all we need to be.

A first step in doing this is to acknowledge the facts: when it comes to human beings, there is no such thing as 'normal'.

An ongoing process

The second key point to take on board is that tackling anxiety, and looking after our mental health generally, is not something we can ever say is done and dusted – it's something we will have to keep on top of for the rest of our lives. Accepting this early in the process gives us a far better chance of making the best progress possible.

There is not a day goes by when I do not do some sort of work on my mental health, be it managing my thoughts, listening to my body or delving deeper into the reasons behind some of my behaviours. It might sound like hell, but it's anything but. In the days when I wasn't managing my mind, I experienced my own personal hell, so I'm well acquainted with what that is like, and I have no intention of ever going back there again if I can humanly avoid it.

Having the ability to tackle my anxiety has given me great peace of mind. It is no longer a huge burden. When I accepted that this is who I am - prone to anxiety, naturally an introvert, averse to change and taking risks - I became more comfortable in being who I am in social interactions, and those situations became easier. There was no longer the pressure to portray myself as someone I wasn't. Most importantly of all, when I was able to stop seeing my brain as a horrible monster and start seeing it as a frightened child who was trying to protect me, it became much easier to be compassionate to myself and push through the negative thoughts. After the initial hard work, I soon embraced my new role as a mediator between my brain and the world.

My biggest hope in writing this book is that it will help those who read it take the first steps along the same path that I, and many of my clients, have followed. In order to move towards greater freedom from worry and anxiety and their limiting effects, it is crucial to cultivate a better relationship with our minds, thoughts and emotions. This, in turn, gives us a sense of ease with who we really are, so that we can actively enjoy social situations and a deeper connection with other people, at work, out in the wider world and in our closest relationships.

Chapter 2
The Reservoir

The vast majority of people who come to my therapy practice seeking help with anxiety do not have any form of mental illness – in the sense that they are not suffering from any kind of serious disorder in their behaviour or thinking. A lot of them would not even recognise themselves as being anxious. They are usually not exactly sure what is wrong, but they know something is not right. They have become overwhelmed and their pre-existing coping mechanisms are not working or are certainly not sufficient anymore. They are struggling and they don't know where to start to turn things around.

When life is going well, everything can seem easy. All the different aspects of our lives just seem to slot into place and little managing is needed. How often do we experience this, however? Most of the time, we are dealing with the worries and stresses of life. So, how aware are we of exactly what we are dealing with? Do we understand how our anxiety works or what causes us the most difficulty? How conscious are we of what we are saying to ourselves? How deliberate is what we are doing to tackle the issues? How do we know if what we are doing is helping or making things worse?

As we touched on in the previous chapter, there are three central aims to this book:

1. It will set out how anxiety and worry work. This will enable you to gain awareness around what areas are causing the most difficulties.

2.   It will enable you to break down your problems into manageable, bite-size pieces and lower the sense of being overwhelmed.

3. It will offer advice and tools to help you tackle the areas that are causing difficulty.

Note that we're not talking about ridding our lives of worry here – we can all expect to be dealing with varying levels of worry throughout our lifetime. Before we progress any further, let's explore this idea of 'worry levels' a little more.

The reservoir

It can be helpful to view our anxiety as the water in a large reservoir. The reservoir is our capacity – emotional, physical and psychological – to cope with whatever life throws at us, and the water is the amount of anxiety we are experiencing at any one time. So, the lower the water level, the calmer and more in control we are. As the water rises, we start to become agitated and life becomes more difficult. As the reservoir gets more and more full, we start to lose control. And when the reservoir is full, we are overwhelmed. Our coping mechanisms are no longer working. Minor things that would not have bothered us when our reservoirs were half-full now cause serious stress. We begin to doubt ourselves and how we ever coped at all: 'What is wrong with me? Why am I not able to deal with the smallest things?'

So, how do we manage the reservoir to ensure that the level of the water – our anxiety – remains as low as possible? Where do we even begin?

If we don't know what fills it up, how do we prevent it from overflowing?

We can't just tackle 'anxiety'. We have to know exactly what we are dealing with. There are many tributaries – anxieties from different sources – feeding into the reservoir. Our goal is to discover where they are and then to cut them off, or at least ease the flow.

This is the essence of anxiety management: becoming conscious of all the areas in our lives where we are most vulnerable to anxiety. Breaking down the problem into multiple, manageable pieces each with practical solutions, and slowly working through the issues. This method will not only bring us back from crisis but will also enable us to maintain a controllable level of anxiety going forward. We need to be able to realise that the reservoir is filling, and not just react when it is already full.

However, no matter how good we become at managing our anxiety, sometimes it just rains. These are the times when things happen outside our control – serious illness, the death of a loved one, a tragic accident. These will contribute greatly to the reservoir and there is not much we can do to stop them happening. At times like these, we need to be managing all our other anxieties as well as we can. We need to keep the levels of our reservoirs as low as possible in order to be best placed to tackle adversity, because if we maintain a low level generally we can better cope when the levels are raised by stress. We do not want to be already overwhelmed when life hits us hard.

It is probably a good time to set expectations here. When it comes to anxiety, we will regularly talk about 'managing', and rarely about 'overcoming'. Whilst we may be able to overcome certain specific fears in our lives – for example, a fear of flying or spiders – anxiety is something that will always be with us to some degree.

As humans, we have evolved to where we are today because of anxiety; it has kept us alert and safe. And whilst we may not be able (or want) to turn it off, we can certainly learn how to turn it down. The focus when we are tackling anxiety should be on integrating tools into our lives to help us recognise and address our anxious thoughts and behaviours when they are not working in our best interests.

So, while the reservoir may never be empty, if we can maintain it at a level that we find tolerable, we are much better placed to move forward and tackle whatever life throws at us.

Tackling the tributaries

Throughout this book, we will endeavour to uncover as many tributaries to the reservoir as possible. We will look at some of the major sources of difficulty and stress in our lives, including work, relationships, our online lives, and other specific areas of worry and social anxiety.

When we are trying to figure out what we are anxious about, it will be important to look at an issue a little more deeply than we normally would. For example, if work is a major source of anxiety, it is vitally important to identify what it is about the working environment that causes such difficulty. It is more than likely not just one thing – and, even if it is, that one thing can probably be broken down into multiple aspects.

Anxiety can be sneaky. It can have us believe we are not actually anxious at all. There may be several things we have low-level anxiety about, but nothing that is causing us to take too much notice. We go about our daily lives, doing the various things that keep our moods in check and enable us to believe we are in control. This can go on for years. But all the while, anxiety is bubbling away underneath the surface. We are able to keep it at bay through distraction and various escape mechanisms, and these just become a way of life. We avoid facing our anxieties head-on, because we are not aware of what it is exactly.

Looking again at work as an example, what exactly is driving your anxiety in this area of your life?

» Do you spend the night before work worrying about what the next day will bring?

» Is your Sunday lost to a sense of impending doom at the prospect of the week ahead?

» Do you tend to overestimate the problem – and underestimate your ability to cope?

» Do you have difficulties saying 'no'? Does this cause you to take on more than you have time for?

» Do you constantly fear getting in trouble or being found out? Are you able to admit when you do not know something?

» Do you need constant validation from others to feel you are doing a good job?

» Do you look back on every interaction, and play it over in your head, focusing on the bits where you feel you made a fool of yourself or said something stupid?

» Has anxiety got to such a level that you cannot start a task and constantly procrastinate, letting your workload build up and become unmanageable?

» Do you see yourself as an adult? If not, how do you see yourself? What is it like working in an adult world when you do not see yourself as one?

From the above questions, you can see that there are many sources of anxiety within one 'problem'.

We are all different in terms of what triggers our worries. However, when we become aware of exactly what we are dealing with, we can start to develop practical steps to address our fears.

If anxiety is something we have to deal with on a regular basis, then we can be pretty sure it seeps into all areas of our lives. Similar questions to those above could have be asked about our relationships, social situations, our futures and how we see them panning out, or any other aspect of our lives. The same issues that may jump out for us in our working environment may also affect other areas. For example, if we find it hard to say 'no' in work, and become resentful or feel taken advantage of, it is not a huge leap to assume this could also happen with a partner or with friends or family members. If we are anxious around social interaction in the office, it's likely that we will also struggle socially to some degree on a night out.

Becoming aware of all the issues in our lives that we have to recognise and deal with may seem daunting at first, but the beauty of it is that, with just a small shift in focus, we can begin to tackle something that has probably seemed out of our reach for a long time.

The tributaries that feed into our reservoirs may be many, but when we figure out what they are, we can begin to get some sense of control over them.

Physical anxiety

There are many different strands of anxiety, each with its own characteristics and triggers, but what they all have in common is how they make our bodies react.

Anxiety is the body's response to situations that we interpret as threatening, and our very distant ancestors would have relied on this response to escape from or fight off wild animals. These days, however, we very rarely need the adrenalin of anxiety to help us in life-threatening situations. Today, much of the anxiety we feel on a day-to-day basis is not physically life-threatening, but has been created in our own minds through worry. It's always future-based, and we are usually imagining bad things that could happen to us or around us. Very different situations – such as the Sunday night before a busy week at work, an upcoming social situation where we might perceive potential judgement from others or a busy bus where we can feel panic coming on – will activate the same response in our bodies that our ancestors used to keep them safe from danger.

As we go about our daily routines, our minds and bodies may be awash with activity, but we are often oblivious to this. If we were asked what we were thinking or feeling an hour ago, we might not be able to say exactly – but that doesn't mean it hasn't affected us. We can be watching TV or absently flicking through social media sites, but our minds are whirling away, generating anxiety-inducing thoughts and our bodies respond in kind, with a physical reaction to the threat of the story we are telling ourselves.

Are you always aware of what you are saying to yourself or what bodily sensations you can feel? Are you even aware of what is going on in your body right now?

As an experiment, let's have a quick body scan to see if we can feel anything. Put down this book for two minutes, close your eyes and slowly move your focus from your toes, up through your feet, ankles, shins, knees, thighs, and so on, until you reach the top of your head. As you move your focus up your body, rest for five seconds on every major area.

Did you feel anything that you were not aware of two minutes ago? Is your stomach tight? Are your fingers tingling? Is your heart beating fast? Do you have a pain in your head? Can you feel a twitch anywhere? Is there any soreness across your shoulders? Might you be holding your hands more tightly than you thought? Are you grinding your teeth?

In order to tackle anxiety effectively, it is just as important to know how your body responds to stress as it is to know what you are saying to yourself. The 'threat system' – or as it is more commonly known, 'fight or flight' – is our bodies' mechanism to prepare us to stand our ground and get ready to fight or, if we don't fancy our chances, to get the hell out of there. Either way, we need to be ready to move. All animals have evolved to react this way to brief and acute distress – something that can be seen in action on the birdfeeder in any back garden. If you watch a small bird landing to eat, it doesn't kick back, pop some peanuts and admire its surroundings. It is hyper-alert, constantly scanning the air and ground, and, at the first sign of any movement, it will fly off. Anxiety is keeping that bird alive.

So, how does the fight-or-flight response play out for us?

Basically, your body prepares itself to address the threat by turning up its emergency functions and turning down the non-emergency ones.

Below are some of the main sensations you can feel when the threat system is activated:

→ Your heartbeat quickens in order to pump more blood to your muscles.

→ Your breathing becomes shallow and faster to take in more oxygen.

→ You may feel dizzy, light-headed or short of breath, as you do not use the extra oxygen you have drawn in.

→ As blood is drawn from your digestive system to feed your muscles, you can feel nauseous, as if you have 'butterflies' in your stomach.

→ As your body looks to drop excess liquids, your bladder relaxes and you may feel the need to go to the toilet.

→ With more blood being diverted to your muscles, your hands may begin to feel cold.

» As you prepare to fight or run, your muscles become tense.

» If you are in a fight for your life or are being chased by a predator, you need to be able to cool down so that you can react as effectively as possible – in order to do this, you may begin to perspire.

» The combined effect of breathing through your mouth and fluids being redirected to priority areas can leave you with a dry mouth.

» As your vision narrows and your thoughts quicken to hone in on the threat, you can feel disorientated and as if your mind is racing.

» If you do not use the adrenalin being generated to run or fight, your body may begin to shake uncontrollably, as the energy that has been generated has nowhere to go.

We all have a similar threat system, but each of us can experience it more intensely in certain parts of our bodies. When I am nervous, I might feel it more in my stomach, whereas you may be more conscious of a faster heart rate or dizziness, or a feeling of being disconnected from reality. Some people will feel cold or need to use the bathroom more, whilst others will shake uncontrollably or get a tingling sensation in their hands. We may be aware of several of the symptoms at the same time. What is important is that you figure out which recurring sensations you get when you feel anxious, with a view to building awareness and tolerance for the physical symptoms of anxiety.

Much of what we experience as stress can be caused by misreading what is going on in our bodies during this fight-or-flight response. As explained, this has evolved to jolt us abruptly into action in situations of acute emergency, so it is not going to feel comfortable. Unfortunately, a lot of times when it kicks off, there is no danger present and so we are just left in our bedrooms with our bodies screaming, 'run!' or 'fight!', but with nothing to run from and nothing to fight. Without understanding what is happening to us physically, we may feel that something is wrong and that we are in danger of having a heart attack, fainting or vomiting and so, sometimes, these bodily sensations will actually intensify our anxiety. We sit there, sensing danger, and, if we don't know what is going on, we may feel as if we have lost the plot completely – it's a very frightening experience.

If this level of anxiety strikes randomly, but on a regular basis, it can leave us feeling out of control, as if we can no longer trust our own bodies. We may begin to be constantly on the alert for these physical symptoms of anxiety and this, in turn, can make us even more anxious. If we go out for a run and our heart starts to beat more quickly and our breathing becomes quick and shallow, this similarity with the symptoms of anxiety can actually cause us to feel anxious, sometimes to the point where we no longer want to do physical exercise. It is not the exercise – it is the misreading of our bodies that is the problem.

Our aim needs to be to get to a place where, although uncomfortable, we can start seeing these sensations for what they are – just our bodies' way of signalling that we are anxious. In the moment, they are not dangerous. We need to use them as an early-warning system to let us know to bring our focus away from whatever it is we are doing and give our bodies and our thoughts a little attention. Depending on the type of thoughts we find, we can choose to respond to them in different ways – and this is something we will be exploring in detail in Chapter 6 – but, in the first instance, we need to acknowledge that we are anxious because we are then in a better position to take action.

So, while the triggers of anxiety may be different for each of us, the physical threat system that is fired into action by the body is the same. Knowing what is happening physically, and that it is not dangerous in that moment, will help us calm ourselves when we are feeling anxious and will mean we are more able to address what is actually going on, rather than being at the mercy of our bodies' emergency responses.

Thoughts

If you are at all familiar with your own anxiety, you will know that your thoughts are often your worst enemy. Constantly dealing with the noise of worry or negativity can be exhausting, but how we deal with our thoughts can make all the difference. We will look at this in more detail in Chapters 4 and 6, but for now we need to learn when to engage with our thoughts and when to let go. Sometimes, we need to bring our thoughts into focus and address them; other times we want to be aware of them, but not allow ourselves to get caught up in them.

To start this process, we do need to know what we are saying to ourselves. I fully appreciate that some people are all too painfully aware of their constant, intrusive thoughts, but this is why we need to make the distinction between the two types of thoughts and decide the best course of action – engage or let go.

Sometimes, examining what is going on in your head and body is the last thing you want to do. Why would you want to take a closer look when you may not like what you find? Unfortunately, however, this is exactly what you need to do. Armed with the information you'll discover, you can do two things. Firstly, you can begin to gain control over how you interact with your thoughts and, secondly, you can learn to use your body as an early-warning system for anxiety, rather than having both your body and mind unwittingly working against you.

Avoiding our fears

While our ancestors' anxiety responses may have been focused on survival, we obviously don't have to worry about the same things today. There is probably a supermarket close by. Predators are not behind every bush. Modern medicine means our health is as good as it can be.

We are, however, hardwired for anxiety, and can

always find things to worry about. Whatever our fears – and they are different for everyone – it is safe to assume that they didn't spring up overnight. Most of our anxieties build over time. If we avoid social interactions, they become more daunting. If we develop a fear of flying, the longer we go without taking a flight, the more the fear grows.

Anxiety is both a blessing and a curse. Without it, we would not survive. However, with uncontrolled or misplaced anxiety, we can be left feeling stuck, isolated, fearful and helpless.

If we ignore or hide from our fears, they will come and find us. This is true of any fear we continually try to avoid. The more we turn away, the bigger the issue becomes, and the smaller we become in its shadow. It doesn't go away. It can't go away. We are shackled to it.

This thing that we are so afraid of now follows us everywhere, and we dare not turn around. And so, the fear grows ever more powerful.

Avoidance

If we spend our lives avoiding the things that would enable us to grow, we end up in a space that is sheltered but limiting. It is comforting but keeps us stuck. It robs us of our potential, and persuades us to stay small, preferring a sense of security over adventure.

We seek to avoid and escape our fears, and the uncomfortable feelings of anxiety that come with them. We immerse ourselves in work or eat to change our mood or spend hours playing video games or looking at porn or we go shopping all the time and spend all our money, or we surround ourselves with people and distractions or we stay up all night watching TV shows or drinking – the list is endless. But everything here serves a purpose and that is to help us avoid feeling what we do not want to feel – in this case, anxiety. The only way to start taking back control is to cast off the need for comfort and distraction, and begin to look out into the world.

Tackling any anxiety is about actively confronting our fears. This doesn't mean suddenly just deciding, 'Right, I have to do everything I'm afraid of right now.' It generally involves a more gradual process, firstly determining what level of fear we can tolerate and then voluntarily – and continually – tackling challenges so that we are always living just outside our comfort zones. No one else can do this for us, and it is only through direct experience that we can move forward. As we spend less time avoiding our fears and start to confront reality more, we slowly gain strength. We prove to ourselves that we are stronger than we might have thought.

Awareness and action

When the realisation dawns on us that we have a problem in a certain area, it can be difficult to admit it to ourselves, let alone to other people. This awareness can, however, spur us to take action and finally address something that we have been avoiding or ignoring for a long time. We may have hit a low ebb and have been forced to acknowledge that we need to change or we may have had some sort of realisation that there is a better way to live. No matter how we came to this place, when we are ready to do something about it, this is a precious time.

It can be difficult to address a problem properly when we don't know exactly what is wrong or what the best action to take is. So, there is an initial figuring-out period. We may talk to others close to us, seek out mentors, do some research online, read books or decide to find professional help. There is so much information available now that, in theory, it needn't take us too long to find the first kernel of wisdom that will set us on our path.

When we discover a source that brings us greater awareness of what we are dealing with, it can become intoxicating. There is nothing like hearing or reading about someone else's experiences that mirror our own, given in words we can understand but have had difficulty articulating ourselves. It is as if that person is speaking about us and directly to us. However, it is crucial at this precious time of willingness to change that we do not get lost in the awareness part of the journey, particularly in this online age where so much information is so easily accessible to us.

The more we find out about ourselves, the more we become hungry for further knowledge. Everyone we talk to will have another suggestion about a great book to read or podcast to listen to. Every YouTube clip that inspires us will have a list of recommended clips for us to watch, and we may find these just as powerful and relevant to our situation. All the while, the initial crisis that caused us to start looking inward becomes a little more distant, and we become calmer, causing the precious window for real change in our own lives to become smaller.

The problem with awareness is that, without action, it can eventually become just another thing to beat ourselves up with. If we have worked out what is wrong with us or that how we are acting is making our lives a misery, and we do nothing about it, the awareness will become nothing more than another reminder of our inadequacies. There comes a stage, pretty soon into the journey of discovery, where action is needed. We must not wait till we feel ready or we have learned all we can about ourselves, we have to get out and start *doing*.

We must decide reasonably quickly when we have enough understanding of our weaknesses, and put one foot forward in an attempt to address them. The worst that can happen in this instance is that we learn something else about ourselves – something we could probably not learn in a book!

Find a 'go-to' ally

When starting out, we need to settle on one person who we feel will be able to support us – someone who has experience in the area and knows how to help us move forward. This person can be a professional, someone online who is an expert in the subject or a friend who has been through something similar and is a few steps further down the road to sorting themselves out.

Do not keep flitting from person to person amongst the very many people out there who are offering help. If you do, this, in itself, can become a distraction, taking your attention away from the real issue at hand. What you need most at this point is effective focus. Aside from this, no one can possibly assimilate in a productive way all the information that is available out there!

We need to figure out what is wrong. What are we currently doing that is not helping - or that is actually making things worse - and what steps do we need to take to start making headway? The handiest place to begin may simply be to stop doing some things that are exacerbating the situation. Then, we can begin - in a gradual, methodical way - to address the fears that we have been avoiding.

Opportunity, curiosity and compassion: reframing anxiety

Anxiety can keep us stuck or it can spur us on. When we come across something that frightens us, do we turn away and hide or do we see it as an opportunity to grow? The fear has obviously highlighted something we are lacking, a skill we do not yet possess or an area of ourselves that we need to explore and develop. We now have a choice about which road we take. Do we look for safety and comfort or do we do something different and try to take steps towards our fears?

It would be so beneficial if we could approach this work with a slightly different mindset. Instead of seeing anxiety as something to push away, can we begin to see it as a perfect opportunity to grow stronger and braver,

and to give us some mental retraining? Instead of being
annoyed and exacerbated when something triggers
anxiety in us, can we be curious and interested as if we
were discovering something novel and important about
ourselves?

If anxiety is a problem and we are looking to change,
then life will give us ample opportunity. When we
become aware of what drives our anxiety, we will
encounter it frequently. Well, we will encounter it
frequently regardless, but, when the awareness is there,
we have a choice about how we interact with it. If we
decide to meet our fears head-on and see them as an
opportunity to move forward, we will be better prepared
and more able to tackle whatever anxiety it is we face. If
we ignore the need to overcome our fears, then, when we
meet them, we will act out of defence and withdrawal,
and will be so much more poorly equipped to handle
the situation.

Curiosity is a powerful tool. When we gain awareness
around an area that was unclear to us, we can begin to
see how it pops up in various aspects of our lives. Let's
say we figure out that people-pleasing is a big problem
for us. When people are not obviously happy with us,
this causes us some degree of discomfort. When we
know this, we will begin to notice it in all our dealings
with other people. If we find it annoying or we begin
to feel helpless, then it is much harder to see this as an
opportunity. If we can approach it with curiosity and
start to think more along the lines of, *Oh, there it is again*

– *that's interesting* or *I didn't realise it was such a big deal for me* or *that it has seeped into so many areas of my life*, then we will be much more open to doing something about it.

Compassion

Learning to tackle your fears will not be easy, especially in the beginning. It would really help, therefore, if you could be on your own side during the process. This may seem like a given, but, in reality, it rarely is. If anxiety is a problem in your life, it would not be a shock to discover that you are also unduly hard on yourself. Having self-compassion can feel unnatural or alien at times, especially if you have spent a lifetime criticising your every decision and downplaying or ignoring your every accomplishment. Instead of deriding yourself, highlighting your flaws and everything that went wrong, can you build in self-compassion? Can you acknowledge how difficult this is and allow yourself to advance slowly and cautiously? If you cannot get to a place of compassion, can you at least stop paying so much attention to the hyper-critical voice in your head?

Self-compassion is a key component to tackling anxiety in the present and managing it going forward. Anxiety is no walk in the park. If we are castigating ourselves for feeling nervous or showing no empathy for times when we really struggle, then it will only make things harder. If a friend or family member came to us with a story of their anxiety, we would probably listen intently and have all the understanding in the world. We just need to find a small piece of that for ourselves.

Finding our motivation

Figuring out *why* we want to get our anxiety under control is just as important as finding out *how* to do it.

Let's consider another aspect of self-care – why do we look after our teeth? The answer is because, if we don't, they will fall out, and look and smell awful. How do we look after them? By brushing and flossing every day, and going to the dentist for regular check-ups. We take this as a given. We can see the consequences of not looking after our teeth and those around us will let us know fairly quickly if we are failing! We're not thrilled about going to the dentist, but we do it and every day we clean our teeth without thinking about it. It's just part of our daily routine.

We have a really good 'why', which makes the 'how' part acceptable.

We need to find our motivation for change when it comes to our anxiety. Turning towards our fears is not fun, even if the rewards are many. But think about what anxiety and worry currently take from your life in the day-to-day choices you make. It may not seem like much but, over time, unmanaged anxiety will take its toll.

What way is anxiety affecting your life? Is it damaging your career or your relationships? What effect does it have on the people around you? What does it stop you doing? Is it detrimental to your sleep, your attention, concentration, mood and self-esteem? Is it affecting how you see the world or is it making your world smaller?

How would things look if you were more in control of your anxiety? What would you be doing that you are not doing currently? How would you be interacting with others? Would you have different goals? The road to managing your anxiety involves facing your fears, challenging your habitual ways of thinking and an acceptance of where you are now. You will also experience the joy that comes with pushing through a fear, the pain of occasional regression and the satisfaction of seeing gradual, long-term progress.

Is remaining in the fog of anxiety, unsure of what is wrong, constantly fire-fighting, using insufficient coping mechanisms and spiralling into a low mood when you become overwhelmed really a better solution?

When we find our 'why', then another great step is to see ourselves as a continual work-in-progress, rather than thinking that, one day, we will be cured or fixed. We will get better and our lives will get easier as we manage our minds and our anxiety, but there will always be difficulties to deal with and we are always going to need to keep on top of our thoughts.

What is the alternative? We can read all the self-help books we want, but if we are not putting things into practice and taking action, we will not get the results we are craving. We can read every night for a year about how to push aside our anxious thoughts and face our fears, but until we start pushing and facing, then it will be for nothing.

It may seem scary, but as we look out into the world, we only need to take small steps to begin. Enough small steps will add up to a minimum of progress. Over time, this will add up to huge change.

Chapter 3
Worry: The Everyday Mindset of Anxiety

Difficulty sleeping. Mind racing. Fears about work taking over time at home. Restlessness. Waking up to face the day, anxious, thoughts whirling. The need to control every aspect of life. A deep fear of uncertainty.

Your mind wanders. You are unable to focus. Your thoughts are awash with catastrophe, danger and worst-case scenarios. Everyday problems suddenly appear urgent, life-threatening, blown out of proportion. Severely doubting your ability to cope, even with ordinary, run-of-the-mill situations, you are constantly tortured with thoughts about upcoming events: *what if, what if, what if . . .*

If you are reading this book, chances are you are familiar with what it's like to be in the grip of worry. It is something that a lot of people have trouble with, though we all worry to varying degrees, and sometimes we can get into a pattern where we begin to worry about all things, big and small.

Worry is a component of General Anxiety Disorder (GAD), but to worry a lot does not mean you have GAD.

When we worry, we often generate seemingly uncontrollable negative thoughts and imagery about future events. In response to the content, volume and repetitiveness of the thoughts, we generally experience a lot of negative emotion, as our brains look to manage future risk, address potential threats and avoid unwanted outcomes. Worry is one of many things that feed into an anxiety that can take over and make life more difficult than it needs to be.

As with the physical sensations of anxiety, worry can motivate us to take action, protect us against surprise, and ensure that we focus our attention on planning and preparation in our everyday lives. When, however, it is done to excess, or is out of proportion with what we are facing, it can be problematic. This is the point at which a manageable degree of worry can cross the line into something that needs to be addresed. We can know that everything is fine and that the current moment is going well, but we cannot stop torturing ourselves with thoughts of impending doom. This degree of worry can make everyday situations feel overwhelming and unmanageable, as our minds constantly reach for the worst-case scenario. It effectively robs us of the present moment, as we spend long periods of time lost in our hypothetical imaginings of terrifying future outcomes.

To struggle with worry is to feel anxious pretty much all the time – with all the physical symptoms that go with it, and which we looked at in Chapter 2.

If we are not worrying, we are trying to avoid worrying (probably unsuccessfully). Intrusive thoughts about health, work, danger, performance, judgement – anything and everything – can be the object of our anxiety, and can include current problems and hypothetical situations.

Those who do not know the power of excessive worry cannot understand why we just can't stop thinking so negatively. On the face of things, everything is going fine, so why worry?

The main elements in worry are:

- ⤏ our thoughts

- ⤏ our perception of worry and the purpose it serves

- ⤏ our own intolerance of anxiety and of uncertainty.

Generally, with worry, something happens that generates an emotional response that we find difficult to handle, and the 'what if' machine takes over.

Does excessive worry equal an excessive volume of thoughts?

If you asked a hundred worriers which one thing they would like to change about their lives, a high percentage would say their thoughts. The common experience of those who worry excessively is that not only do they think in a way that drives them crazy at times, but the sheer volume of their thoughts can often feel overwhelming. Because these thoughts are so worrisome, and because they spend so much time caught up with them, the worriers presume that they are generating a much greater volume of thoughts than other, 'normal' people. The truth, however, is that our thoughts are not behaving as we would like, and we are just paying them much more attention than they deserve. It is the content of our thoughts and the nature of our responses to them that makes them seem excessive and overwhelming.

If you asked two people who had just driven through the centre of a busy city to estimate how many traffic lights they had encountered, there might be two very different answers, depending on the level of engagement of each person during the drive. If one person was stressed about being late, cursed every red light and beeped their horn at every intersection to try to get other drivers to move more quickly, they might come up with a higher number than another person who was under no time pressure and simply enjoying the drive while listening to music they love. The truth is, of course, that both drivers encountered the same number of traffic lights, but, as the second person wasn't paying as much attention to them, they imagined there were fewer. Likewise, if every worrisome or intrusive thought you have is met with fear and a sense of annoyance, which feeds into your churning stomach or fast-beating heart, you may believe that you are having an unusually high volume of thoughts – but this isn't actually the case.

Clickbait

You're no doubt familiar with the term 'clickbait' – those sensationalist, often misleading internet headlines that grab our attention and draw us in to reading the fuller content of less-than-important stories. The way we interact with our worrisome thoughts can involve a very similar process. Our mind is always telling us some kind of story, but it isn't always one with a great deal of truth to it, or very much substance at all. Like many clickbait headlines, our anxious thoughts may present themselves to us as significant or interesting – but so often, they really aren't. Our thoughts might seem important – after all, they emanate from us – they are 'our' thoughts, and therefore they must be significant, relevant, accurate, right? How about meaningful or urgent? We certainly seem to treat them that way.

'What if I can't pay the rent and I get kicked out of my apartment?' *Oh, that looks like a story I might be interested in.* Click!

'What if my constant tiredness and fatigue mean something serious about my health?' *Yes, what would I do if that were the case – I'd better have a closer look at this one.* Click!

'What if I lose my job and can't get another one?' Click!

'What if I'm not as attractive as . . .' Click!

'What if . . .' Click! Click! Click!

It is generally the energy we spend dealing with our anxiety-generated thoughts that causes us so much difficulty. More often than not, the harder we try to resist them, the more persistent they get. The more we try to push worrisome thoughts away, the more difficult it becomes to concentrate at work, which can then increase our anxiety and distress. The more time we spend in our heads with our worries, even when we are away from work, the less present we are with our friends and family, whose company could be a potential source of relief. The more we cannot tolerate anxiety-provoking thoughts, the more likely we are to engage in behaviours of escape – such as using social media, food, porn and alcohol – which will give us momentary relief, but cause us more problems in the long run.

The reality is that we don't have more thoughts than a 'normal' person, we just pay them more attention, and react to them in a way that is counterproductive.

We'll explore ways that help us pay less attention to our worrisome thoughts, and deal with them in such a way as to turn down the volume on them. The bad news is they're not going to disappear any time soon – but the good news is that we don't have to give them the credence we currently do.

The trap of seeing worry as a positive

There are times when we worry so much and our thoughts are so intrusive that it feels like we're going crazy. We can't get a break from our heads. Day after day brings the same routine of poor-quality, interrupted sleep, a tense, nauseous stomach, an inability to concentrate and that horrible feeling of being overwhelmed. At these times, worry can be such a negative in our lives – which is why it is strange that we often find it so difficult to let go of. Although the thought of constantly living with it drives us to distraction, there may be part of us that fears life without our worry.

Many worriers have common misconceptions, which means that they can represent worry to themselves in a more positive light than it really merits. We can believe that worry got us to where we are now or that we would become complacent or overconfident without our tendency to worry, and so we perceive value in it. After all, it keeps us safe, as we never let our guard down – so why would we want to give it up? Often, it is the uncertainty of who we would be without our excessive worry habit that can lead us to putting up with the pain.

As we have seen in Chapter 2, there is no doubt that anxiety can be a necessary driving force in keeping us out of harm's way and helping us prepare for the unexpected. We study for exams, look both ways when crossing the road and don't put ourselves in unnecessary danger – and there is clear value to all of this – however, there is a big difference between being practical whilst allowing an element of risk, and constantly worrying and fretting over every little thing.

As much as it may feel like a positive, excessive worrying does not serve any purpose other than to tie up valuable 'head space', when we could be doing truly useful preparation, relaxing or engaging with our loved ones. The reality is that constantly worrying about the future does not mean we do any better when we actually get there. Our constant, fretful 'what ifs' about that presentation at work may actually mean that on the day, we are tired, our thoughts are all over the place and we are probably overprepared. Instead of trusting that if we write a few bullet points, we will be able to talk confidently about something we know, our excessive tendency to worry throws up an image of ourselves on the day going completely blank and being humiliated in front of a group of people. So, we end up writing out the entire script of what we will say, which will undoubtedly make us less relaxed and less fluent when we come to speak.

So, if we are still caught up in our own heads and preoccupied with worrying, it is highly likely that we will not be fully present to deal with whatever it is we have spent all this time fretting about should it actually come to pass. This would suggest that worrying has no real benefit, other than to rob us of space where we might be doing something more productive, more relaxing or of more value to us.

The truth is that we have made it to where we are *despite* our worry, not because of it. It has not been helpful to fret unduly or wake up in the middle of the night and immediately obey the urge to write a list of things we need to do in the morning. Worry can seem like problem-solving, but do we sit down, work through a problem and come up with a solution in a timely manner? Or do we flit in and out of our thoughts, whilst trying to distract ourselves from the worst-case scenarios our brain is concocting?

Constantly overthinking every little thing does not help us move forward in the world, nor does the attempt to control every aspect of our lives help us plan for the future or give us the certainty we crave. If we routinely try and think of every eventuality and figure out how we would deal with each one if it arose, we can soon develop a mental habit whereby our brains see overthinking as a way of keeping us safe from uncertainty.

Where would we be if we didn't engage in this practice? My guess is in the exactly same place we are now, only having had much better sleep and with fewer grey hairs!

Uncertainty: worry's jet fuel

Everything we do carries an element of risk, because – unfortunately for worriers – nothing in life is certain. We can make lists, plan everything to the last detail and try to think of every possible eventuality, but this will only get us so far, offering at best the illusion of certainty. As Voltaire once said, 'Uncertainty is an uncomfortable position. But certainty is an absurd one.' If we insist on control, and try to avoid uncertainty altogether, our lives quickly become very restricted. We look only to the familiar, reluctant to push out into the world and do anything that brings with it any element of the unknown.

The focus of our worry may change, of course – it may be work today, relationships tomorrow or our health next week – it is, however, not the content of our thoughts that is important; the problem is not knowing what is going to happen and not being able to tolerate that uncertainty.

We often think that if we just knew how things were going to play out, we would be able to relax. We might indulge in the fantasy of winning a large sum of money and the belief that this would sort out our uncertainty around financial security. A devoted partner, who was 100 per cent compatible with us and with whom we'd never argue, would surely take care of relationship worries. Knowing in advance and with 100 per cent certainty that we were going to live a long and happy life would mean we could calm down about our health and safety. But all of this is illusory thinking, of course, and when we step back out of the fantasy each time, the reality of uncertainty is still there, waiting for us.

No matter how many times we come up with rational answers to our continual 'what if' questions or how many times we get reassurance from others, our brains will have something else in store that has an element of uncertainty attached. For example, think about the scenario where your finances are under pressure, and the limitless negative thoughts you could indulge in around this fact.

What if I can't make it to the end of the month and payday?

What if I can't afford to go out on Saturday night?

What if I can't pay my bills?

What if I can't get my credit card debt under control?

What if something happens to the car out of the blue and I can't afford to fix it?

What if I can't afford to get away this year?

What if I lose my job?

What if, what if, what if . . .

Repeat ad nauseam.

How do we answer every question? Where does it all end? Each thought is a natural progression from the last. The 'what if' rabbit hole is bottomless. We worry about so many things that never happen – but the fact that they don't happen doesn't stop us worrying.

As we have said, it is our burning desire for certainty that is the breeding ground for worry. In the same way that a damp room is the perfect environment for mildew to thrive, the need to control everything means that anxieties can only multiply and grow. Of the people who come to my practice looking to get their worry under control, those who grudgingly accept that they have to learn to build tolerance for uncertainty are always in a much better place to succeed. No amount of work we do on ourselves will give us certainty. It is the ability to live with uncertainty that enables us to get worry under control.

Tackling uncertainty

Before we do anything with regard to accepting uncertainty, we need to acknowledge to ourselves, with compassion and curiosity, that our endless need to predict and prepare is a real problem. It is one thing for us to believe that we just like to be well prepared and have an element of control over things – but there is preparation and then there is wanting to control every last detail and think about every eventuality.

When we admit to ourselves that we cannot tolerate uncertainty, we can begin to do something about it. 'This is me. This is what I do at the moment. I don't particularly like it, but I've obviously developed it to protect myself somehow. Maybe it isn't helping me much any more.'

As with all of this work around anxiety, if we can park any self-criticism or judgement as much as possible, then it will immediately remove a considerable potential obstacle from our path.

Preparation versus worry

When we start to tackle uncertainty, we often have difficulties around separating good, common-sense future preparation with unnecessary, excessive worry. If we learn to listen to what we are saying to ourselves, we can begin to decipher one from the other.

Take exams, for example. We want to be concerned enough so that we do adequate revision, get proper sleep, turn up on time for the exam and generally do our best. However, when we start worrying so much that we cannot study, then it becomes a problem. We might find ourselves thinking of the mountain of work we have to do and wonder how we will ever be able to get through it all in time. We think about our peers and how easy they seem to find it all, and about the possibility that we will do really badly in comparison. We think about never being able to get the grades we need, perhaps even concluding that there's little point in trying in the first place. We imagine our friends and family feeling pity for us or feeling let down by our woeful performance. We think about how we will feel about ourselves, as we are probably our harshest critic.

Our thoughts might take us further into the future, as we wonder what will happen if we can't get into the career we want, or progress to the next level of our current career, so that we end up being left behind by our friends. Maybe our minds begin to speculate on how this may affect our potential relationship prospects or our ability to be happy in life.

Before long, every time we think about the exam, this avalanche of thoughts is set off, engulfing us in full or in part, which means that we find it impossible to sit still and study for any length of time. We begin to procrastinate, doing anything to take our minds off the situation. We find that using social media works a treat, and this soon becomes a pattern. We spend more and more time with our chosen means of escape, because of the temporary respite we get from our thoughts and the uncomfortable feelings. We continue to worry about the exams and to waste valuable time, and we can't stop either one.

After a while, we may find ourselves at the mercy of a feeling of impending doom that we do not even realise is about the exams any more. This sense of dread just lurks in the back of our minds and rolls up from time to time, like the tide coming in. The anxiety continues to go unaddressed and may soon become a pervasive low mood. Now, we are feeling down and the troubling thing is, we can't explain to ourselves or others why.

As we can see from the example above, excessive worry over uncertainty, coupled with the burning desire to get away from the feelings it produces, is not a great combination. In this type of situation, our thought processes and methods of escape may become so familiar – since we have used them in so many other contexts – that they have become a fixed pattern of response, a template we can just fit to any situation that we find threatening or potentially overwhelming.

Observing yourself

You can start addressing such unhelpful patterns by observing yourself over the next week or so, with a view to becoming more familiar with how you worry and how you try to deal with uncertainty.

If you are more aware about your mind and body, you will be better placed to step in when the worrying begins, rather than feeling awful and not knowing what is going on. You need to listen out for the 'what if' questions, check if your concentration levels have dipped or if you are in a period when you are easily distracted.

As covered in Chapter 2, if we get used to paying attention to our bodies, we can begin to recognise what it feels like when we are worrying or feeling anxious. We are trying to listen to our bodies' cues, with a view to knowing when we are lost in worry.

We all have many thousands of thoughts per day,

which fit broadly into themes, and this is the case with our negative thoughts too.

It is really helpful to be aware of them and name them as they come in. When you catch yourself grappling with uncertainty, with your thoughts going down the all-too-familiar rabbit hole, try to give a label to those thoughts – for example, 'future worry', 'uncertainty thoughts', 'control thoughts', 'what if thoughts' – whatever you like. For example, if you are in the early stages of a relationship and your thoughts keep running ahead of you with fears about things not working out, call them 'relationship worries'. If your thoughts keep playing out worst-case scenarios around current salary, paying rent and never being able to afford a house, label them 'financial uncertainty'.

In Chapter 6 (Anxiety Toolbox II), we will look more closely at how to tackle the intrusive nature of anxious thoughts, but, for now, we just need to become aware of them and observe them doing their thing.

We are trying to identify times when we worry excessively. We are not going to throw out our sensible preparation for the future, but we are looking to work on the areas where the desire to control the future becomes counterproductive.

So, we are aware that uncertainty is a problem, we are beginning to learn how our bodies feel when dealing with it and we recognise the general thoughts that come with the territory. The exact content of those thoughts will change frequently, but the theme will always relate to our sense of a lack of control over a future event.

Next, we need to acknowledge to ourselves some basic facts about our existence – mainly, that nothing in life is certain. Uncertainty is our reality, and trying to control every outcome will only serve to feed in to our worry by letting our brains know we cannot cope and that they need to continue to send the 'what if' thoughts to protect us.

I'm not saying we have to like it, but if we are at least aware that when we attempt to control every aspect of the future, we are trying to change the fabric of reality, we can begin to open up a small space in our minds to the possibility that what we are doing is futile.

Seeking reassurance

When trying to tackle the beast of uncertainty, there is one mental habit in particular that it can be beneficial to pull back from.

When our tolerance of uncertainty is very low, it is common for us to seek reassurance from other people. We might have a 'go-to' person whom we always run things past or maybe we just check in with anyone and everyone, from family to work colleagues to random people on the bus. Either way, this is another response that tells our brains that uncertainty equals danger, and that we are not to be trusted with decisions.

Again, though, this is something we need to look at in terms of balance. If we occasionally turn to colleagues to bounce an idea off them or we look to family when we are making a major decision, then this is prudent and a natural thing to do. When, however, we are constantly doubting ourselves and turning to others to make decisions for us or to validate our choices, then this can quickly become problematic.

The more we hand over decision-making to someone else, the more we feel that this is something we must continue to do. The self-doubt this engenders becomes more and more deeply rooted and, very soon, we do not trust ourselves with smaller and smaller decisions. At work, where we once only asked for reassurance in relation to complex decisions with no clear path forward, we now turn to colleagues for everyday decisions that we didn't think twice about before. Again, it is this process of letting our brains know we are not comfortable with uncertainty, coupled with the fact that there is uncertainty in everything we do, which makes it a natural progression to our not being able to make *any* decisions for ourselves.

This can be a tough one to undo because we did not get to this place overnight. It was a step-by-step process, and that is how it will look in reverse, as we seek to back out of the situation we now find ourselves in.

As with all our work tackling anxiety, the way forward is to face our fear and start with small steps in the right direction.

If we have an inconsequential decision to make, our brains may tell us: 'Just run that by someone first – it'll only take a minute.' A long-standing pattern of complying with this kind of response lets our brains know that we regard the danger as real, and that it was right to send the thought. What we need to do now is to acknowledge the thought (because we can't stop it), and make a conscious choice to go with our own decision anyway. This will feel scary – but that is to be expected and it's why we start small. We want to show our brain that we do not agree with its diagnosis of danger, and that we see the situation as less relevant than it does.

When you first start this process, your brain will immediately object and ramp up the anxious thoughts: 'What do you mean, we're not getting reassurance? We always get reassurance. Don't be crazy – just run it past someone quickly!' As you observe yourself not seeking reassurance and surviving, your brain will slowly begin to come on board and will eventually stop sending its danger signals.

Initially, you need to catch yourself in the process of handing over a small decision to someone else, and observe how you deal with the situation. What are your thoughts before you reach out to the other person? When you seek the reassurance, how often does the answer you're given differ from your own instincts about the matter? You may find that you almost always concur with the third party's take and so should conclude that the reassurance was unnecessary.

Sometimes, however, we are so used to passing on decision-making that initially we are a little shakier and not always clear about what our own instincts actually are.

When we observe how we tend to react in these situations, it is about forging ahead and making the smaller decisions, without seeking reassurance going forward.

We have to make these choices on our own, all the while acknowledging the risk that they may not be the best choices. We cannot expect perfection because to do so will make getting the decision wrong a failure, rather than a potential opportunity for learning.

As we slowly gain confidence in our own decision-making, we begin to take more responsibility for our choices and actions, and rely less on others for guidance. We are able to start tasks without going through every detail with other people, and can trust in ourselves to figure it out as we go.

Pushing forward into uncertainty

As we start making our own decisions and observe ourselves living with small amounts of uncertainty, we can push on in other areas of our lives.

It's trial-and-error stuff – finding out what works for you and what doesn't, as you step carefully out into the unknown.

As stated earlier, we need to be conscious of our pre-existing belief that if we don't plan for uncertainty and worry about everything, our lives will fall into chaos. As we continue to challenge that belief, in small ways at first, we begin to build trust in our ability to handle the unexpected. Ultimately, the only way to get more tolerant of uncertainty is to encounter it continually and voluntarily. If we expose ourselves, voluntarily, to things we have previously avoided and are afraid of, we get stronger. Of this there is no doubt.

In this process, we may observe that, if given the choice, we will often pick a negative outcome over an uncertain one. The reason for this comes down again to our long-held need for certainty – because, at least with the negative outcome, we know the result. We can put it to bed. It's the same reason that someone may leave a job they are in because the uncertainty of not knowing how they are doing becomes too much for them to handle. They would rather have no job than be in a job they could possibly fail at. Again, the problem for such people is the undefined – the possibility that they could fail, not the failure itself, which would at least bring certainty. Conversely, this may keep someone in a job they hate, because they fear the uncertainty of a move: 'what if it's worse?' We can see from this just how limiting the fear of not knowing an outcome can be in our lives.

We must learn to become more accepting of the reality that uncertainty is a natural part of life. We cannot avoid it. Unfortunately, the only way is to face it and go through it. This process involves gradually exposing ourselves to low-level uncertainty – uncertainty that causes some discomfort and triggers a small amount of worry but is not too much for us to handle. For example, you may be someone who worries excessively about going into town on a Saturday afternoon. If so, you might deal with this by planning the day down to the last detail: bus times, weather checks, choosing a lunch venue before you go, and so on. Unless this is an extremely challenging situation for you, you could start with just going into town and seeing what happens. The idea is to drop trying to predict every possible outcome. Trust that, whatever crops up, you will be able to handle it.

As we start experiencing more, and avoiding less, we begin to gain confidence. Choose something relatively simple to begin with, and just give it a go. Remember to take it slowly. If you feel you need support, find a counsellor or psychotherapist, someone impartial who can support you through this process. But just start. The whole point is that we prove to ourselves that we can handle obstacles in our lives, including what can often be the biggest obstacle – uncertainty.

The idea is to progress through our higher level fears, when we have mastered the lower level ones, always living on the very edge of our comfort zones, since constantly pushing our boundaries is where real growth happens.

Chapter 4
Anxiety Toolbox I

O f the clients who have sought my help with anxiety, without exception, the ones who have progressed the fastest and gained the most control over their anxiety are those who have been willing to do the work between sessions at home and on a daily basis.

Those who take on board - and take responsibility for - the process of owning and managing their anxiety and are willing to incorporate the learnings and techniques from our sessions into their everyday lives are always the ones who will reap the fullest benefits of this work.

To do the work, we need the tools. This chapter is the first of four throughout the book that will introduce you to the contents of your Anxiety Toolbox - which will be an invaluable resource as you take control of the problem of anxiety in your life.

The Toolbox – Parts I, II, III and IV – will bring together some of the strategies and techniques that have proven most effective and most useful to both myself and my clients over the years in managing anxiety.

In this chapter, we will look at the tools and strategies of mastery, the daily check-in, writing your thoughts and playing with the timeframe.

In the same way that the experience of anxiety itself plays out differently for each of us, each of these tools may resonate differently with you – and what works well for one person, may not for another. So it's a good idea to try them out, and pick and choose those that best suit you as an individual and the way you prefer to work.

When you have built some awareness of what areas in your life are most dominated by anxiety and have some tools to help you in this work, it's time for action!

Managing our expectations

This first tool is actually a way of thinking – a mindset – rather than a practical technique.

When I initially came across it in my own personal journey, it instantly clicked with me and made sense of why I always seemed to start so many things but never saw them through. I have also found that it has greatly helped many of my clients to take a more measured approach to managing their anxiety, enabling them to relax into a process that they could be forgiven for wanting to rush.

Many of us have had the experience of starting new things – the gym, learning a foreign language, yoga, online courses, piano lessons, and so on - only to find that, after the initial burst of enthusiasm, we just as quickly lose interest and give them up. What's happening here is that we want to change something - usually an unwanted, recurring feeling - and the exciting new venture does exactly that - initially. It gives us a quick jolt of, 'This is what life is all about!', and then reality kicks in as the new activity becomes difficult, mundane, too time-consuming or generally a hassle.

When we are looking to do work on ourselves, this same pattern - the initial enthusiasm followed by a slump in interest and motivation - can be especially evident. This is where unrealistic standards and expectations of constant progress can stop us achieving our goals. More and more, we look for the quickest way to get what we want. The thought of something taking large amounts of our time and commitment is off-putting. We want to be good at the new skill the minute we start - and if we are not, we don't see the point of trying at all. If we are anxious or a worrier, then sticking with a commitment may be difficult, as we can't be sure how things will turn out. There is nothing that feeds uncertainty, and therefore worry, like not progressing as well as we think we should be.

Driven by our own standards of how we think we should be performing, we can have a belief that we must always be visibly progressing, and, when we are not, this can feel very defeating. It's the feeling of not progressing that can make us quit and this, in turn, can lead us to think badly of ourselves, as our thoughts turn to how useless we are and how inevitable failure always is for us.

What many of us don't understand, however, is that progress is hard to measure accurately if we are just using how we *feel* we are doing as our gauge.

In his bestselling book, *Mastery: The Keys to Success and Long-term Fulfilment*, George Leonard, the renowned US author and educator, outlines what real progress towards being good at something difficult and worthwhile actually looks like. When learning anything, the initial burst from 'zero' – no knowledge or ability – to 'knowing something' can be quick and thrilling. If we are learning to play a musical instrument, for example, being able to put together a few notes can give us a buzz of excitement and the feeling that anything is possible. The learning process becomes more problematic, however, when we expect this upward trajectory to continue at the same rate and our progress to look like the line below.

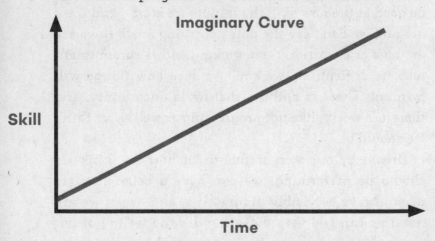

What we expect mastery to look like.

As we continue with our learning, however, the excitement swiftly diminishes, and we are faced with the reality of the journey ahead of us. As the initial fun, our keenness to learn and the sense of novelty begin to fade, we quickly realise that things are not going to be easy.

Leonard believes that mastering any new skill involves short, sharp bursts of progress, each of which is followed by a slight dip and then a plateau for a certain period of time. Real progress, he argues, is gradual. It can feel slow, sticky and boring at times. Yes, there are moments when progress is tangible, but most of the time we are in practice mode – so the real progress curve, Leonard asserts, will look more like the line on this page.

In this diagram, there is still an overall, upward trajectory, but most of our time is spent on the plateau, churning through the mundane, repetitive and

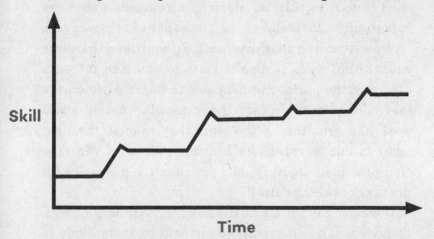

What real mastery looks like.

sometimes unsatisfactory work, until we get to the next spike, after which our progress tapers off again.

The plateau can get a bad rap in society today. We are made to feel that if we are not constantly achieving, winning and taking big strides forward, we are not focused enough or simply not working hard enough. However, the truth is that, in this type of work as in many others, we have to pay our dues on the plateau to be able to make any strides at all. The 'winning' is a tiny moment in time. The plateau is the constant.

If we start something new or set ourselves a goal, we want to experience continuous, visible progress. If we don't, we feel like we're failing – and it is this feeling that can cause us to quit. But giving up on our goals can have a detrimental effect on our mental wellbeing. Much of our positive emotion around achievement comes from being able to see that we are moving towards a goal. And if we don't have any goals, we are denying ourselves so many opportunities for feeling a positive sense of achievement.

When learning anything that is difficult, and therefore worthwhile, we have also to learn to embrace setbacks as part of the journey and be able to tolerate life on the inevitable plateau. In fact, the plateau is where the real work happens, this is the work that enables the next jump in our learning. As Leonard puts it in *Mastery*: 'You practice diligently, but you practice primarily for the sake of practice itself.'

If we get caught up in the need for visible progress, then we will be disappointed and will be more likely to give up.

If we think of any goal we've achieved in our lives, we will see the truth of this. Nothing worthwhile is ever achieved instantly or painlessly. When we reach our goal, there is a momentary high, but then there is tomorrow and the next day. So, in this sense, the high is fleeting anyway. Life moves on. Very soon, we need a new goal and, to achieve it, we must also force ourselves to take the sometimes laborious, sometimes boring but always necessary steps along the way.

It is, however, on the way to the goal that life is lived. The slow progression can give us an enormous feeling of satisfaction but only if we can let go of the need to see constant progress.

Mastery in context

If we take our working lives, for example, we can see that progress in the workplace operates in the same way. There may be new jobs, new roles, promotions and so on, dotted throughout but, in the main, we are on the plateau. Not as in, 'Oh no, my career is plateauing!', but the place where we just knuckle down and get on with our jobs. We have an eye on our goals but, mainly, we are simply doing the work.

Since we often don't realise the impact we are having in our workplace, we can presume that what we are doing is going unnoticed. We don't *feel* like we are progressing. What we need to do here is to allow ourselves to learn, practise and become proficient in what we do. As we have already said, achieving real, tangible goals requires a lot of work that is mundane and unassuming. We are not always going to be the standout person in the room.

When it comes to anxiety, it can work the same way. With the initial awareness and the decision to take concrete action, there is often a positive, buoyant feeling. Soon, however, this learning process becomes like every other, requiring practice, patience, persistence and time spent on the plateau, honing our tools. With this kind of work, allowing ourselves to feel comfortable on the plateau is crucially important because of the sheer strength of feeling anxiety can cause. Those who live with anxiety want the feeling gone, and quickly – but this is not how this process works. Managing anxiety is something we need to incorporate into our lives, even when it feels like we are not making any progress. If we can keep in mind Leonard's principle of mastery, where the skill we are mastering is the ability to manage our anxiety, it will be so much easier for us to knuckle down for the long term and accept that the most worthwhile goals always involve time, setbacks and commitment.

Daily check-in

If we've been habitually ignoring difficult emotions for as long as we can remember, how we are feeling and thinking may often be a mystery to us. The tendency to operate in a hazy fog is something worriers may be very familiar with, as they try to do battle with thoughts they'd rather they weren't having. However, before we can do any useful work in managing anxiety, and our mental health in general, it is crucial for us to be able to pin down our thoughts and emotions with as much clarity as possible.

Asking yourself how you are and how the day has gone is a good practice to build into your daily life, and can have a three-fold benefit. Firstly, particularly at the beginning of this work, it will give you a sense of what is and isn't helping when it comes to the strategies you are trying out to better manage your anxiety. Secondly, keeping in touch with your inner self in this way will help you build the capacity to address or let go of difficult thoughts, and to deal with any painful emotions that need addressing directly. Thirdly, over time, a daily check-in will help you realise that facing how you are feeling is not as scary as you perhaps once believed it was.

Making this check-in or review part of your daily routine doesn't need to be a big deal – you just ask yourself a few simple questions, so you know if you are in good shape or if you need to do a bit of work. Anchoring your check-ins to something you do every day as a matter of course can be really helpful, as piggy-backing on an existing habitual event makes the check-in easier to remember and incorporate into your daily routine. Something that has worked very well for me and my clients has been to use morning and evening tooth-brushing sessions for this purpose. We tend to brush our teeth on autopilot, and it is something that we know we will be doing at least twice a day. It's also an activity that offers the perfect brief window of time for a quick check-in. Of course, if you find something that works better for you, then go for it! Perhaps it could be during your commute to work or while eating your lunch or as you wait for the kettle to boil for your usual afternoon cup of tea – whatever is best for you.

For example, in the morning as you brush your teeth, simply ask yourself how you are. *How do I feel today? What have I been saying to myself since I woke up? Is there anything I've been mulling over in my head that needs to be brought into the light or is there a persistent thought that I need to just acknowledge and let go of?*

When you brush your teeth at night, it's a similar routine. *How am I now, just before bed? How did today go? Was there anything that caused me any difficulty that I need to address quickly? Is there anything I did today to tackle my anxiety, and was it helpful? Do I have anything on my mind that is likely to affect my sleep?*

This check-in does not need to become a huge burden, where we drag up all sorts of unwanted feelings. It's just a brief check-in. If we think there is something that needs further examination, we can set aside time later in the day (or the following day) to address it more closely. Then, at the designated time, we can see if the feeling is still as intense or if we can just let it go.

We go about all of this in the same way we would if we woke up with a sore throat. We wouldn't immediately presume we were sick and needed to reach for medication – we'd wait a couple of hours, and possibly put it down to how we'd slept. If then we felt better later in the day, we could afford to just ignore it on this occasion. If, on the other hand, the pain remained, then we'd probably need take a closer look. So, if there is something that pops up in the check-in, we can write it down if necessary, give it the morning, or sleep on it, and see if the troubling thoughts or emotions linger. The check-in should not extend beyond the boundaries of the daily process we have anchored it to.

In Chapter 6 (Anxiety Toolbox II), we will look at how to address the common types of thought that tend to come up for us, but, for now, it is enough to use our daily check-in to get a general sense of what is going on for us. The idea is that we are getting more comfortable with asking ourselves how we are, and are not too afraid of the answer.

Writing to think

Sometimes, in a therapeutic setting, people are fully engaged and speaking fluently about things that have happened to them or about thoughts they have had about the previous session. More often though, people look off into the distance, reaching into their thoughts and tentatively saying words they hope make sense. They are thinking, and the act of talking out the thoughts helps them formulate what they really mean or feel. They are often surprised at what emerges, since they weren't previously aware that they had these thoughts or that the thoughts in question had such a depth of feeling behind them. It's an amazing process to be part of and, in those moments, a therapist will stay out of the client's way as best they can. Any interjection at that stage can pollute the process, taking the person out of their thoughts or leading them to add details or reflections that do not belong there.

Writing down our thoughts can afford us a similar opportunity to slow down for a moment, focus our minds and aid the thinking process. This can be such a powerful tool. When we are stuck in our thoughts of worry or anxiety, we can go around in circles for hours without any kind of resolution. It's often only after we get the thoughts out of our heads that we realise what is really going on. Writing down our thoughts can do this for us and give us a clarity that we cannot get through thinking alone.

So, especially at times when anxiety or worry seems to be taking over, try writing down what is going on in your mind. At the very least, it will slow down your thinking and provide some perspective. You can then read over what you have written and look at it more objectively, which can spark another stream of thoughts.

Next, you can analyse how you are thinking or step back from your thoughts and come up with solutions or input that may have been unavailable to you earlier. As you read your own words, you can try to come at them from another perspective entirely. *What would I say to another person who had written this? What advice would I have? Would I understand what they were going through? Would I be sympathetic to their situation?*

As you are writing, try free association. Just write whatever words come to mind. Nobody else will be reading what you write. You don't need to censor yourself or worry about punctuation, grammar or spelling. Simply try to write about what you are feeling at that moment – your hopes and fears. It is OK to not know what to write

- just put down whatever your brain says. If it bores you, write about being bored and see where you end up. If you think it's a stupid exercise, write about what it feels like to be wasting your own time . . . Just write, and follow where the pen takes you.

In Chapter 6 (Anxiety Toolbox II), we will be looking at a process to enable us more direction in dealing with and challenging some of our thoughts, but, for now, writing freely is a simple process to help us think. Keep it simple and stay out of your own way.

Playing with the timeframe

Playing with the timeframe of our thinking is a really good way to get more control over worry. Sometimes, our thoughts are so far off into the future that they lose all sense of reality, yet they still fill us with dread. At other times, we are so closely focused on how we feel in the present moment that we lose sight of the bigger picture showing how we are doing overall. In the first scenario, the future worry can be all-consuming; in the second, the moment-to-moment feelings can be overwhelming.

If we are at work and have a project or a large, complex task to deal with, we can often race off in our thoughts to a time days, weeks or months down the road, and a scenario where we have failed miserably to get the work over the line – people are angry, our reputation is damaged and our current job and future job prospects are in jeopardy. Here, we are completely underestimating our own ability to cope and risk getting seriously stuck in this future worry.

At such times, what our brains need more than anything is to observe us starting and making progress. With the making of progress, our worry lessens and our brains turn down the critical warning signals. Unfortunately, however, worry and anxiety can make it difficult to start anything, as the uncertainty becomes too much to handle. So, we put off starting anything, and if we continue to do this, we will end up proving to our brains that it was right to worry!

This is where the timeframe in our minds needs to be seriously pulled in. When we catch ourselves worrying about things too far ahead into the future, we need to call out the thought ('future worry'), and calmly bring ourselves back to the present moment. When in the present, we then make a deal with ourselves on how far ahead our worrying thoughts are allowed to go: 'I'm just going to deal with the next two hours. Anything beyond that is not something I can control. I'm going to live with the uncertainty and deal with starting this task.'

Now, these aren't magic words and your brain will probably still head off down the worry road, but you keep reining things in. Every time you catch your worry running farther ahead than it needs to, you do not engage with those 'future thoughts' and you gently guide your mind back with compassion and without judgement.

Picture a puppy straying farther away from you than feels safe. Pick him up, bring him back, rub his little head and tell him, 'Just stay close to me for the next while, as I finish what I'm doing just now.' If you don't like dogs, use whatever imagery works best for you!

What is important is that you have a relaxed sense of control over the timeline and you stay, as best you can, inside the boundary you've set yourself.

When it comes to how we are feeling, we sometimes need to pan out and see a larger timeframe. This is especially useful if we are particularly intolerant of feeling uncomfortable emotions or if we tend to make the fact that we are having a difficult time mean something about our futures.

When we are feeling low or anxious, it can often be difficult to get out of this frame of mind, but playing with the timeline is really worth trying. If we are having a bad few hours or days, and our worry feels particularly intense, it is very helpful to pull back and ask ourselves how the past week or month has gone. OK, perhaps this particular day hasn't gone great, but maybe the week overall has been good. So, this can offer the perspective that things are not going as badly as we think at that moment, and also give us a sense of the impermanence of any particular mood or emotion.

To help with this tool of expanding the timeframe of our thinking, it can be useful to start tracking our daily moods. We can do this in a simple paper diary, or use technology in the form of a mood tracking app, of which there are many. The advantage of the technology option is that we can visualise a timeframe much more easily. We can often look back and think that we've had awful week in terms of worry because negative emotions tend be more difficult to deal with and stay longer in our memories. A bad bout of worrying before bed can risk clouding an entire day that may have been perfectly fine. We can easily forget that the week had many good moments or had full days when we felt fine. If we make note of our moods every evening before bed, we have really helpful data to use when we are not in a great moment. This tracking should only take thirty seconds, with just a few words – the more cumbersome it becomes, the less likely we are to do it.

Playing with the timeframe of our internal dialogue when things are difficult can be a really effective tool. If a worrisome thought hits us and gets our anxiety going, we can ask ourselves why we are feeling this way now. If we were perfectly fine twenty minutes ago, and nothing has changed, why are we letting this thought dictate how we feel now?

So, we pull the timeframe right back and refuse to engage in anything too far into the future. Using this technique in conjunction with some of the tools in Chapter 6 can help us to distance ourselves from these unconstructive future thoughts and not get too caught up in some of our more difficult thinking patterns.

Chapter 5
Socially Anxious

It's Saturday evening, and you've arrived at the front door of the house where the party is being held. You check your phone to make sure you've got the right address - yes, this is it. You were really pleased when your colleague invited you earlier in the week - you don't know her very well, but she seems like a nice person and is always friendly and good fun at work. You're usually pretty shy and not really a party person but you know it would be good to go, to push yourself to get out and to have some fun - even though as Saturday got closer, you started worrying about it all, the way you always do about this kind of thing.

Now, as you're standing here on the doorstep, you know this is the bit you normally hate - walking into a house, and most likely a crowded room, where you'll hardly recognise anyone, added to which, you have no idea what to expect from the evening. Finally, you pluck up the courage to ring the doorbell.

When the door opens and you're shown in, you immediately go into a heightened state of anxiety. As you desperately try to look composed, your brain is shouting 'run!', your heart is thumping and your thoughts begin to race. Your fight-or-flight response is well and truly engaged, your brain is flooded with thoughts and your whole body is primed for danger, to enable you to make the split-second, life-or-death decisions necessary to help you survive an imminent, deadly threat.

Only you're not in the path of an on-rushing tiger or an assailant with a machete – you're just standing in somebody's hall, about to go into their front room – and so this panic reaction isn't all that useful. You have been building this up in your head for the past few days, thinking about how it could go wrong and all the things you might do to embarrass yourself, with all those people there to see you and judge you. And now you are finally here!

You enter the sitting room and see a group of people chatting and laughing. Although you know some of them, the fear of approaching them is all-consuming, but you have to do something – you're standing on your own in an empty space in the middle of the room and people are looking. *What if I say 'hi' and nobody acknowledges me? What if they wonder why I am here or who asked me to come? What if I was just invited as a nice gesture, and they never thought I would actually turn up?*

You quietly say 'hello' and stand at the edge of a

group. As one person turns to talk to you, your focus goes inwards and you scan your body for signs of visible anxiety. As you feel your cheeks flush, a sense of panic descends. You feel excruciatingly exposed, and are convinced the other person must be aware of how anxious you are. Although you've talked to this person a few times at work, you can't remember their name. Then, an avalanche of thoughts kicks in, as you try desperately to think of something interesting to say, whilst simultaneously ruling out anything that occurs to you as not good enough.

You've known how to stand since you were a toddler but suddenly you can't for the life of you figure out where your hands and arms should go. *Where would normal people put them? I'm so weird.* You shift from one foot to another, never being able to settle on a position that feels – or, more accurately, that you think looks – natural. You are sure the other person is aware of this and is already regretting turning away from the fun to chat to you.

Just two minutes have passed – but it feels like a lifetime.

Someone else in the group asks how you are and what you've been up to since you last spoke at work, a week or two previously. You reply with a simple, 'Fine'. It's such a short time since you last chatted, but your brain is in pure survival mode and you don't have access to memory. To take the focus off yourself and try to buy some time, you immediately ask them how they've been. As their reply seems to be coming to an end, you haven't listened to a word they've said – you've been too busy desperately trying to think of something else to say that can save the situation – and you draw a blank. You mumble something about having to get a drink in the kitchen and they turn back into the group. When they sign off with, 'See you later', you blurt out, 'You're welcome.' *Arrrrrrrgh!*

As you make your way to the kitchen, the post-mortem is already in full swing. Once again, it confirms everything you already think about yourself, as it always does. The awkwardness, the inability to talk, the fact that people find it hard to interact with you. You cringe every time you think of what you said and how you must have looked. As you enter the crowded kitchen, your nightmare continues.

You spend the rest of your evening wondering how soon you can leave without insulting the host. *How can I get to the toilet without having everyone look at me as me walk awkwardly across the room? How will I eventually leave the house – will I have to say 'goodbye' to the host and everyone else? I haven't even said 'hello' to most people. What on earth will they think of me?*

Walking home, you dissect the entire thing and play it over and over in your head. You were just at the party for a couple of hours, but the experience stays with you for days afterwards.

Take this situation and transpose it to a queue at the bus stop, lunch at work, the supermarket or any other everyday scenario that a socially anxious person finds threatening – and it will play out in the same kind of way.

Fear around social situations is extremely common, though the degree to which this can affect our lives varies. Some of us are more comfortable, and feel safer, in one-to-one situations where we can listen to and connect with another human being, but will feel terrified by the exposure and potential judgement of a group. For others, the group setting is not a problem, as it enables them to engage on a non-personal level and keep their true selves relatively hidden. In the intimacy of a one-to-one conversation, however, they can be painfully awkward, as they presume the other person does not want to be there and they may feel somehow responsible for the 'success' of the interaction.

This chapter cannot tackle the complexity of social anxiety, but it aims to give those who struggle in social situations some perspective on the problem, on how we can contribute to it (or at least how we do not help ourselves) and what steps we can take to begin to feel more comfortable in the company of others.

If you feel social anxiety is interfering in your life to an untenable level, or for a more in-depth look at the issue, I'd recommend Dr Gillian Butler's excellent book, *Overcoming Social Anxiety and Shyness*, or find a good therapist who specialises in this area. If you find social situations problematic, but not crippling, then there may be enough here to get you on the path to better engagement. In Chapters 7 and 8, the two chapters that deal with anxiety in the workplace, we will also look at some more specific, work-related social situations and how to cope more easily with them.

In our personal lives, social awkwardness or ineptness can keep our true selves hidden, as we present a persona to the world that we hope will somehow be acceptable. In today's professional environment, having good communication skills is an important element of most jobs and a crucial attribute in terms of gaining promotion. We humans are social animals, and difficulty in this area of our lives can be very restrictive.

Very rarely can people who struggle with social situations point to one incident, one defining moment, where it all started. Developing social anxiety is usually a gradual, unseen process that can creep up on us, like ivy slowly inching its way up a tree. It can take over our lives before we realise what is happening. Every time we avoid a social situation, we confirm to ourselves that we cannot cope. Every time we make an excuse and leave a group situation or stay still and silent in a group discussion, our fear around all of this gets bigger. If we lock ourselves away and keep our dealings with other people to a minimum, it is obvious that this will have an adverse effect on our ability to deal with human contact going forward. It will also deny us opportunities for meaningful and potentially fulfilling interactions with others – from which they might get something too!

Unhelpful assumptions

In Chapter 2, we talked about how avoiding our fears only serves to make us more fearful in the long run, and it is no different when it comes to anxiety around social situations. However, why is it that, even if we push ourselves to maintain regular contact with others – in the workplace, during nights out and in broader life in general – our fears around social situations do not seem to go away? There are a number of factors that play into this that we need to be aware of before we can really begin to turn things around.

One of these factors is our tendency towards unhelpful assumptions – the way we think about social situations plays a huge part in maintaining our fears. We overthink every situation before it occurs. If we have a social event coming up or a presentation to do at work, we picture ourselves making awkward conversation with people who would rather be anywhere else than with us or we imagine ourselves going completely blank in front of an expectant audience. Whilst most people experience fear, nervousness and apprehension at times in their relationships with others and have had bad social experiences, the difference for those who are socially anxious is that we actively *expect* the situation to go badly, every time. We think ourselves into such a state of dread that by the time the event comes around, humiliation seems inevitable. It is this expectation, coupled with the belief that we will always be judged harshly by others, that makes it hard to experience any social interaction as it truly is, and not as we have built it up to be.

This presumption – of disaster and inevitable social rejection – means we are more likely to perceive judgement and negativity, regardless of what actually happens. We are looking for it, and therefore we will find it. We assume we know what the other person is thinking, and interpret non-verbal cues as proof of our assumptions. If someone looks away for an instant, this indicates that they are not interested, a sigh means that they find us annoying or boring, a gap in the conversation is proof that they do not want to be there and it is either our responsibility to say something fascinating to gloss over the silence or to take this as our cue to leave this poor person alone. Behind this expectation that the interaction will go badly often lies some more deep-seated belief that we are somehow weird or different or that we will always come across as awkward, spaced out or somehow not 'normal'. Everyone else is socially literate, except for us.

Too much internal focus

Another aspect of this unhelpful approach to social situations is that, rather than focusing on the person or people we are talking to, we are internally focused, completely caught up in how anxious *we* feel or how *we* must appear to others. If we can sense our hands shaking, our voice trembling or our underarms sweating, we presume it is also obvious to those around us. If we feel our cheeks flush, we imagine it is all the other person can see, and that our face is lighting up the room. We do not look out into the room to gauge how people are actually reacting to us; instead, with all our attention directed inwards, we presume they see us exactly as we see ourselves in our own minds.

Punishingly high standards

Another factor that commonly feeds into the difficulties socially anxious people have in interacting with others is perfectionistic thinking and the incredibly high standards they tend to have for themselves in public situations.

In Chapter 7 (Anxiety in the Workplace – Part One), we will be looking in detail at the impact such perfectionism can have at work. However, even when it comes to less formal settings and purely social interactions, our expectations around what we contribute in casual conversations are often so ridiculously high that we cannot possibly hope to meet them. If what we say is not observably funny, interesting, intelligent, and so on, then we feel we will not be acceptable. Others cannot possibly just want to be with us for our company – we feel that we must bring value that is explicitly acknowledged (whether in the form of laughter or an agreeing nod), since our mind is just waiting for the first opportunity to tell us that we are not good enough. We cannot just chat and let the conversation come to us. Everything we think we might say will be run through a filter which will determine if it is good enough for our audience. This means that very little of what we could contribute is allowed to escape from our mouths, which can leave us racking our brains, desperately looking for an acceptable answer to a relatively easy question. This, in turn, gives our inner critic all the ammunition it needs to continue its ongoing narrative that we are a social disaster: *I couldn't even answer a simple question. What is wrong with me? What must people think of me?*

Safety behaviours

One of the biggest barriers to experiencing social situations as safe and non-threatening is the use of what are known as 'safety behaviours'. In Cognitive Behavioural Therapy, a safety behaviour is something we routinely do to protect ourselves from our feared catastrophe. When we are in a social situation, these behaviours can be many and varied. They can be pre-emptive measures, which help stave off the fear, or things we do when the feared situation has occurred. The most obvious and most commonly used one is avoidance – simply not going to the meeting or the night out or a friend's party.

Safety behaviours before a feared social situation might also include:

➤ Getting there early, so we can scope out the environment and see people coming in, thus eliminating surprises

➤ Always having someone with us, so we do not have to walk into a situation on our own

➤ Sitting close to the door in a meeting venue, so that we can leave quickly if necessary

➤ Having a bottle of water at all times, so that, under the pretext of taking small sips, we can get momentary breaks from the proceedings, and feel more comfortable in having something to actually do

» Preparing interesting things to say before entering a conversation

» Leaving our coat away from our desk, so we can leave work without having to say goodbye to people.

When we are actually *in* the feared situation, common safety behaviours might include talking very quickly or in a low voice, so that the focus never stays on us too long.

If we are aware of having symptoms of anxiety, such as shaking or blushing, we may hold our hands very tightly under the table so people cannot see the tremor or try to cover our faces, so those around us do not see our awkward mouths or red cheeks.

While safety behaviours might bring the illusion of safety, in reality they simply help to maintain the fear. They offer relief in the moment, but do not enable us to experience the event as non-threatening, as, if things go well, this will most likely be attributed to the actions that we believe keep us safe. If, as we walk along the corridor at work, we resort to scanning the screen of our phones while walking to avoid interaction, we not only miss the opportunity to see that interaction need not be scary but we also confirm to our brains that the situation is indeed dangerous and, but for the phone, we would not get through it. This only reinforces the need to keep the safety behaviour going.

The post-mortem

Finally, when it comes to unhelpful habits that serve only to perpetuate our worst anxieties, the pièce de résistance of the socially anxious person is the brutal and unbalanced post-mortem that we invariably indulge in after the feared event is over. Negative, anxious thinking has dominated the lead-up to the social situation, completely hijacked our ability to relax and be ourselves during the interaction and, now that it is all over, is only too ready to rush in with judgement about our perceived performance. And guess what? The verdict is not good – naturally!

We go back over the things we said and did or how we think we looked. We use the bogus data we have gathered through our skewed perspective as evidence of how poorly we managed the situation and how badly everyone must think of us. We focus on our own physical feelings of anxiety to gauge how terrified we must have appeared. We process the non-verbal cues we picked up from others to confirm that they found us boring or pitiful. We draw on our unfounded assumptions that other people are so much better at social interactions than we are, to attest to our own weirdness and, from all of this, we finally conclude, once again, that we just cannot be trusted in a social situation.

As we can see from all of the above, although we may continue to engage in interactions with other people every day, we do not get the benefit of that exposure because of the processes and ingrained thinking that we have developed around such situations. We do not become more comfortable in encounters with others, even though we appear to be constantly facing our fears. This is because with our fearful thinking patterns, our safety behaviours, our skewed, entirely self-focused perspective and our deeply held beliefs about ourselves, we are not really facing our fears at all – at least, not in the sense of putting our hands out to hold a spider or stroke a snake. By holding on to our old thought patterns, we are never dealing directly with a real social situation, but only ever with the faulty template in our heads, which we place over reality like a filter – and which ensures that so many of these situations always turn out the same way.

If we presume they won't like us

If we suffer from social anxiety, our processes around social situations are often so convoluted that we remove much of our true selves from the final picture. What is left is a Frankenstein's monster of what we think we should be, what we think will be acceptable, what we think will not offend, what we think will please and what we think will go unnoticed. Whatever this thing is, it is not us. 'It' is not the person that those we know well would recognise, and the truth is that often other people, those who don't know us, don't know how to interact with 'it'.

Think about how you would approach someone who

you know doesn't like you, versus someone who you know is a friend. You would very probably approach the first person in a closed, cold and defensive manner, whilst you will be open, friendly and relaxed with the second. Each of these people will experience a completely different version of you.

The problem with social anxiety is that you can assume people who do not know you well will not like you. People who are met with this version of us will inevitably pick up on our coldness, and, inadvertently, change the way they interact with us – when, in fact, it was our own approach that has left them unsure about how to act around us.

We hate to look awkward or tongue-tied, and yet concentrating on how we are standing or filtering everything we say, can make us look exactly this way. If we fear people do not want to be with us, we will be constantly pushing them to leave, making them feel that we do not value their company, when this is far from the truth. We may fear coming across as boring, so we keep our responses as brief as possible, yet we are not actually offering anything for the other person to work with, so they may indeed lose interest quickly. We don't want to be seen as a nuisance or annoying, and yet, in talking in a low voice or very quickly, in order for the focus to be moved on from us, we may actually draw more attention to ourselves, as people cannot hear us properly. In this sense, there is a self-fulfilling prophecy element to social anxiety, which only adds to the complexity of our fears in social situations.

How to start moving forward

As I said at the beginning of this book, much of my knowledge about the issue of social anxiety is derived from my own experience and that of my clients. It is with this understanding that I have been able to engage with some of the best work out there on the subject. For example, British psychologist David M. Clark has developed a great Cognitive Therapy model around social anxiety. Some of the practical strategies I draw on when working with my clients are very much inspired by Clark's research. As stated earlier, however, if social phobia is something that is taking over your life to an unacceptable degree, then you will need more than this chapter can offer – at the end of this book, for example, you will find a recommended reading list with suggestions for further reading, including details about some of Clark's publications.

We have identified the roadblocks, so now we have to figure out how best to move forward. As always with this kind of work, this will be a process of trial and error – having an experience and deciding what we can learn from it, and how this in turn feeds into what we already know. Tackling anxiety in social situations is all about being able to get to the actual experience, with all the noise of our thoughts, beliefs, presumptions and safety behaviours cut away. Otherwise, we are never actually facing the fears in a way that enables us to garner any real learning from the experience.

Breaking into the old process: awareness

Once again, being aware of what is happening is a good place to start tackling the problem, and what we have considered so far should have given you some insight into how anxiety can play out in social situations.

In this first stage, we need to think, in particular, about the things we do socially that we believe keep us safe. When we know what our safety behaviours are, we can observe how they work for us (or, more accurately, how they don't work for us). Next, we need to think about what it would feel like to drop these safety behaviours and still go into a social situation . . . Terrifying? Achievable? Or both?

Now, we are going to look at some practical strategies to help us break away from our old processes.

Stop feeding the troll

Our thoughts play a massive role in ramping up and maintaining anxiety around social situations, and so a key part of breaking unhelpful patterns is to try to better manage our thinking.

We could do battle with our hypothetical fears and unfounded beliefs, telling ourselves that humiliation isn't inevitable and that, while experiencing the feared event might be frightening, it will be manageable, and so on. But probably a more beneficial way to deal with our thoughts in this context is to simply try to engage with them as little as possible.

In some ways, our minds are like the internet. There is so much good stuff available online – so much valuable information, knowledge and potential for learning – but our attention is constantly being distracted and pulled away by nonsense. If you have spent any time on social media, you will most certainly be familiar with the term 'troll'. An internet troll is someone who likes to start arguments and upset people, purely for the sake of argument and upset. They are not looking to add value, engage in good faith or have a meaningful discussion.

With social anxiety, our thoughts are definitely troll-like. They are ready to take us down at any moment with a disparaging comment – or a barrage of unhelpful speculation, negative beliefs and unfounded fears. Here are a few examples of how this can play out:

Me: I might go and visit my friend later.

Mind: *He doesn't want to see you. He has other, more important things to do. You'll be a nuisance.*

Me: I'm looking forward to going out tonight.

Mind: *You look like shit – people will notice and stare.*

Me: I'll go over and talk to that person.

Mind: *You'll come across weird and awkward – they'll think you're strange. Don't do it!*

Me: I think I'll go for that promotion.

Mind: *Don't bother, you'll never get it. You're no*
             good at your job and everyone knows it. If
             you let it be known that you wanted the
             promotion, it'll be even more humiliating
             when you don't get it.

Me: It'll be great to see my colleagues at the
             work Christmas party tonight.

Mind: *Nobody wants you there. They all think*
             you're soooo boring!

Now, what's the worst thing you can do with a troll?
Engage with them.

They are craving your reply. The troll is dying for you
to respond because, when you do, they have you – and
the really destructive work can begin. They are fishing
and you have just jumped on the hook, again!

What's the best way to deal with a troll?

Ignore them.

It doesn't mean that what has been said doesn't hurt. It
doesn't mean that you won't want to jump in and defend
yourself, dispute the comment or dwell on the upset. It
doesn't mean the trolling thoughts won't happen again.
But it does mean that it can end soon for now, and you
can concentrate on something of actual value to you.

This is exactly how we should treat our anxious thoughts.

The you're-weird-not-normal-not-like-everyone-else-not-good-enough thoughts. *Do not engage.*

We can acknowledge the thought to ourselves by naming it - for example 'Troll Thought' - and then let it be. It is when we try to resist or fight this kind of thinking that it tends to get dug in.

I appreciate this is not that easy - no doubt you have been caught up with your thoughts for as long as you can remember. In Chapter 6 (Anxiety Toolbox II), we will delve further into the best way to bring about this separation of ourselves from our thoughts, through a process called 'defusion', which has been borrowed from Acceptance and Commitment Therapy (ACT).

lower our standards for social performance

Since human beings are social animals, the majority of us care what other people think of us. So, practically everyone is dealing with some level of fear around judgement and wants the impression they make to be a positive one. Those of us who are anxious presume that the world is looking at us with great scrutiny, but the reality is that everyone is so caught up in their own heads, most often they barely notice what is happening with us. Neither is everyone as judgemental and unforgiving as we fear. Perhaps we have a few standout memories from our past, when we found that we were the centre of attention for all the wrong reasons, but we cannot live our lives with the presumption that a repeat performance is inevitable.

As an experiment, observe a conversation amongst a medium-sized group of people. Listen to what is actually being said. I guarantee you that there will be people talking absolute nonsense, and nobody will bat an eyelid! Things that would never get through your filter are being spouted off all the time and everybody is totally fine with it. But how do these people get away with it, if the group is such a judgemental tyrant? Because maybe it's not. Maybe people don't expect every conversation to be perfect. Maybe it's actually the off-the-cuff, imperfect interjections that enable everyone to say whatever they want to say in the first place. If we are socially anxious, we need to get over the idea that everything we say has to be funny, intelligent or engaging to be acceptable – but it is only experience that will give us this reassurance.

Throughout the rest of this chapter we will look at how to start gaining that experience.

Put away the radar

If we believe humiliation and judgement are inevitable, we are more likely to see them when they are not present. We need to stop believing in our ability to read meaning into everyone's actions. We need to stop reading into non-verbal cues. We do not *know* what they mean. When people look away, sigh, yawn, tap their feet, and so on, it could mean any number of things. It is not always about us. Can we put the radar away?

A neutral take

We really need to think about how we are presenting ourselves when we are in social situations. If it is difficult to fathom how people might like us, can we at least enter into a conversation with a neutral view of the other person's opinion of us? It is likely we do not know what they think.

If we approach people from this perspective, we will be less defensive and more likely to show sides of ourselves that others can relate to. The other person is not trying to catch us out, and we are not looking to confirm our own beliefs by monitoring their reaction to our defensiveness. If we learn to approach social interaction from this position of neutrality, we are more likely to experience these as less negative.

I feel anxious, therefore I look anxious

One of the biggest fears of the socially anxious is the idea of appearing anxious – a fear that others will be able to tell that we are having difficulty, that it will be obvious to people that we cannot cope in social situations or are easily embarrassed. We need to break the link between the physical sensations we feel when we are anxious and a belief that others will inevitably notice these and associate them with our being nervous. We also need to break the link between the possibility of someone noticing we are nervous and our automatic assumption that this will make them think badly of us.

During a social interaction, it is definitely more difficult to manage our thoughts, because we are in the lion's den, so to speak – under the spotlight. Our anxiety has kicked in and we are in survival mode. In truth, the feelings and physical symptoms we have are not as noticeable as we may presume. They feel very intense to us, so we presume they are visible, but this is so often not the case.

It's very important that we look outward into the room more, so that we can gauge what is actually going on, rather than what we expect to be going on.

When we look inward and focus on what we are feeling and thinking, we are at the mercy of our inner monologue. We then lose sight of the evidence that is in front of us, and, instead, use vague impressions, feelings and our anxiety to read the situation. We also need to remember that, even if some people do notice that we are nervous, the judgement we fear is either not there or is so much less severe than we might imagine.

Fair and balanced post-mortem

As has been outlined, a highly self-critical post-mortem plays a crucial part in maintaining our social difficulties. Now that we know what we are doing, we have a choice about whether or not this is something we will continue doing. I know it's not a case of 'just stop doing it' – it never is with anxiety – but we can make other choices now. We may not be able to stop the post-mortem, but does it need to be as horribly biased against ourselves? Does it need to be as cruel?

It may feel alien to be compassionate to ourselves, but we can surely get to fair. If we were in a court of law, the judge might not be friendly, but he or she would probably still be just. When dissecting a social event after the fact, we have to try and bring some balance and fairness. Can we decide that we will only use the facts, i.e. what we know to have actually happened? That would be a good starting point.

It is so important when going over how a social interaction went, that we stick only to the evidence we have available and keep away from the non-verbal cues. Again, if we look at it from a legal point of view, what we think someone else might have thought would not be admissible as evidence. If we didn't get unambiguous feedback from those we were talking to, we actually have no idea what they were thinking, so we have to stop pretending we do.

If we have to do a post-mortem (which we don't, by the way), can we try and do it as if we were talking about someone else, someone we care for? Would we be so harsh? Would we ignore the evidence, and berate the person for being so awkward, stupid, abnormal, etc.? Or would we be more balanced and understanding?

Time to experiment

Now that we have the awareness and are working on changing our mindset, the most powerful thing we can do is go out and experience ourselves surviving social situations.

To do this, we need to go into situations that scare us, whilst gradually dropping our safety behaviours. This requires us to be operating just outside our comfort zone and pushing ourselves to a degree that is enough to be a challenge but not so far as to be unattainable.

We then set up experiments.

We have to know what we are testing and we have to be clear which safety behaviours we are going to drop, in the knowledge that they do not actually keep us safe, they merely keep us stuck. We also need to know what success looks like.

So, for example, take the struggle to speak up over lunch at work. You may fear you will come across as boring or stupid, so usually you think of things to say before you sit down with the group (safety behaviour A), and eat very slowly, so that you are not sitting around doing nothing and feeling exposed (safety behaviour B). If you step back from this situation, you can think about how to test your beliefs – in this case, the habitual assumption that, 'If I talk in the lunch group, my colleagues will perceive me as stupid or dull.'

Next, you need to decide how you will recognise judgement from others. It cannot be something abstract – such as you imagining what is going on inside someone else's head – it has to be a tangible sign, like someone rolling their eyes or sniggering when your point is not intended to be funny. You also need to decide how you will gauge if the interaction is a success for you. A reasonable evaluation needs to be something like, 'If I say something and the conversation continues as before, with no major reactions, then I will see that as a successful contribution.'

As you go into the situation, you must consciously drop your safety behaviours. This is a crucial part of the experiment. Therefore, you do not think of things to say beforehand, you simply trust that you will be able to react to the ebb and flow of the conversation. You make sure to eat your food at your usual pace and, when you are finished, look out into the group, ready to participate. When there is an opportunity to speak, add something you feel like saying, and then see what happens.

After the event, you need to come away and have a think about the experiment you have just run. You have to bring the 'fair post-mortem' principle into play and stick only to the actual, discernible evidence. You will be going to lunch all the time, so you can run the experiment again and again, changing elements and pushing yourself a little more on each occasion, so you can get an accurate sense of what people really think about you when you say something in group conversation.

It is good to get into the swing of running such experiments on a regular basis, within various social situations. When you begin to challenge your beliefs about yourself and others, you will soon get a sense of when and to what degree your thinking is seriously off-kilter. What you will very likely discover is that people aren't as harsh and unforgiving as you thought.

Maybe your humiliation is not inevitable. Maybe you are not as weird as you feared. Maybe you even have something to offer.

Chapter 6
Anxiety Toolbox II

Wherever we go, we can be sure that our thoughts will be with us. Is there ever a time that they stop? Even when we sleep, they are whirring away, feeding our dreams. They wait - sometimes patiently, sometimes less so - for us to wake up and engage with them in our usual way. Wanting them to stop is an unrealistic and unhelpful wish, as they are never going to. As we saw in Chapter 3, those of us who worry a lot often think we have more thoughts than the average person, but everybody has roughly the same number per day, so it is not the volume that is the problem, or even the overridingly negative content of worrisome thoughts, it is our emotional reaction to them that can make them seem louder or more frightening. Over time, if we learn to give these negative thoughts less attention, they will become quieter and more infrequent.

There are, in fact, no thoughts that you could have that other people haven't had. Your mind is just throwing a string of words at you and, if you don't react, your brain will move on to the next random thought. If you have a strong emotional response and try to fight off the thought, you are letting the brain know that its content is in some way relevant and that there may be danger. So, in an attempt to protect you, your brain will keep feeding you this same thought.

In Chapter 5, when we talked about 'troll thoughts', we discussed just how effective it can be to simply ignore the troll!

To challenge or let go – that is the question

When we are looking for ways to address our thoughts in a different manner than before, it's important to be aware that not all of those thoughts should be treated in the same way. There are generally two broad categories of thoughts, which require two very different responses. Sometimes we need to shine a light on what we are thinking and step back and think about it logically; at other times, we need to simply acknowledge the existence of our thoughts and then just let them be. Some will quieten with a rational response; others will feed off our attempt to rationalise them, and see this as a confirmation of their importance.

As we continue to expand our awareness of what we are thinking – and this will be achieved with commitment and practice– we will become more adept at recognising which category a particular thought or thinking pattern falls into. In this chapter, we will look at ways of making these distinctions and at techniques for handling these different kinds of thoughts.

For thoughts that can be challenged, we will be looking at 'Thought Records', a tool used in Cognitive Behavioural Therapy (CBT). This technique helps us to drag our thoughts from the hazy fog in the back of our minds and out into the light of day, so we can see what we are dealing with and bring some balance to our thinking. For intrusive, speculative, 'worry' thoughts, those which dwell on situations that haven't yet happened (and often never will), we will be using a process called 'defusion' – a component of Acceptance and Commitment Therapy (ACT) – with a view to separating ourselves from our thoughts.

Firstly, however, we need to know which thoughts to challenge and which thoughts to defuse.

Thoughts to be challenged

The thoughts we need to bring forward and challenge are generally those that have an element of uncertainty to them, ones that relate to a specific, concrete situation we are dealing with, or that we may have to deal with in the near future. If we have a closer look at the context of such thoughts, we will see that we have a lot of relevant information already available that we are currently ignoring. These are not the recurring thoughts that we are always grappling with, but tend to be negative thoughts around specific situations. We've allowed the problem to niggle away at the back of our minds, unaddressed, because it is uncomfortable to look at. We may be distracting ourselves with one escape method or another to avoid thinking about the issue but, in reality, we have handed it over to our negative thoughts to get to work on. And get to work they will!

Some anxious thoughts thrive in this vague and foggy space. Whether you are paying attention or not, your brain is continually mulling over the issues you are worried about. If you have been experiencing negative and worst-case scenario thinking for a long time, then defining and challenging our thoughts is an approach that will be used here. So, if you have just had an argument with your partner, or are worried about a work interview coming up, these are some scenarios where you can challenge your thoughts.

To give you an example: say you are due to go back to work after a long period off sick, and you are worried about what your manager and colleagues might think and how you will cope with their reactions, not to mention the more demanding aspects of your job after so long away. This is a thought, or a train of thought, that would be helpful for you to examine more closely – What specifically are you worried about, etc.? – and then go about challenging, so that you can see the problem in a more rational light. This, in turn, will enable you to think about whether you are possibly overreacting in your thoughts and about concrete things you could do in order to make your transition back to work easier.

We'll be unpicking this particular scenario more on page 103, when we look at Thought Records.

Thoughts to let go

If our thoughts are intrusive and persistent in nature, where the content is purely hypothetical and filled with danger, trying to challenge them may keep them alive, by letting our brains know we are seeing the thought with its hypothetical scenario as a real threat. For example, if we constantly worry that a relationship will not last, even when our partner continually shows us love and is always reassuring us, then this is a thought that would be better served by less attention, not more. Or if we are continually worrying about what our colleagues think of us and assuming that it will be negative, no matter what evidence we have to the contrary or how many times we have talked ourselves around, then this is also a thought that might just need less oxygen.

If we are unsure which approach to use, we can play with both and see how the thoughts in question respond. It is only when we experience our thoughts quietening, becoming more balanced and less intrusive, that we will gain trust in a certain way of responding. Do allow for a decent trial period, as this will all be new and, however unhelpful the old ways of thinking may be, your brain will initially prefer the easily accessible, well-worn tracks your worry habit has laid for you long ago.

Thought Records

Cognitive Behavioural Therapy (CBT) has many great tools for helping us address anxiety and change our old ways of thinking, and one that has been of great benefit to both myself and my clients is the Thought Record. This enables us to get unhelpful thoughts out of our heads and down on paper where they can be examined and challenged. It can be a great way to ease our anxiety about a given situation and an incredibly helpful tool that we can use to bring reason and balance to a situation where our negative thoughts have been given free rein.

When we talk about what makes us anxious, or what we are worried about, it is so important to get our hands dirty in the specifics of what exactly is going on. Using broad categories, such as 'work' or 'my relationship', to initially identify what aspect of our lives is troubling us may be a good way to open up a process of reflection – but to make any real progress, we need to dig down further into what specifically in those areas is causing us difficulty and how exactly are we reacting to it.

A Thought Record can help us step back from a spiral of negative thinking, by walking us through a process where we can gain much-needed perspective. It is not about positive thinking or looking on the bright side of life, but more about helping us find a voice for the other side of the argument in order to come to a more balanced conclusion. Negative, catastrophic thinking might have had the upper hand in our minds for the past two hours; now, we are just letting the other side have a chance to respond.

Thought Records can be used before we approach a situation that we are unsure and worried about or after an event to look at what has been causing us difficulty, and to stop a brutal, unbalanced postmortem in its tracks.

There are seven key elements to a Thought Record:

1. **The situation:** What happened or what is about to happen?

2. **My emotions:** What you are feeling? Rate the strength of each emotion as a percentage, from 1–100 per cent (where 100 per cent is the emotion at its most intense).

3. **My thoughts:** Write down everything you can about what you were/are thinking. Identify the thoughts that are causing you most pain. Get it all out and save no paper!

4. **Evidence for my thoughts:** Just because it is negative does not mean it is untrue. You are not dismissing your thoughts out of hand, as to gloss over reality is not the goal here. Simply list the evidence that supports the negative thoughts, so you know what you are dealing with.

5. **Evidence against my thoughts:** This is where the challenging of the negative thoughts will happen, as you note down all the evidence that doesn't support them.

6. **Balanced thought:** Having taken into account all of the above, come up with a new thought

that takes in both sides of the argument and is as close to the truth as you can get to with the evidence you have.

7. **My emotions:** Now you reassess each of the emotions from Point 2 on the previous page, again rating them on a percentage scale. It's important to note that they will very likely not have disappeared altogether, which is fine. The goal of the Thought Record is to lower the intensity of the original feelings.

The beauty of Thought Records is that, the more we do them, the easier they become, and the more we can incorporate them into our everyday thought process. In time and with practice, we will develop the capacity to use a Thought Record during an actual situation and not just in hindsight, so that we can learn to lower our emotional responses on the fly, so to speak.

As we have seen, there are all sorts of situations in which we might use a Thought Record. Here are two examples that use Thought Records before and after a situation or event.

EXAMPLE ONE

SITUATION

Had an argument with my partner an hour ago.

FEELINGS

Angry: 75 per cent; Frustrated: 60 per cent;

Helpless: 40 per cent; Anxious: 30 per cent

THOUGHTS

I can't believe my partner could be so hurtful.

Why can't they see my side?

Will we ever be able to work things out?

They wouldn't say those things if they really loved me.

They don't care about me.

Why am I even in this relationship?

This is typical of all my relationships.

I'll never be happy with anyone.

EVIDENCE FOR MY THOUGHTS

What was said really hurt, and my partner always says hurtful things when we fight. They stick to their argument and don't budge, even when they hear my side. When they are angry, they don't seem to care that I am upset.

EVIDENCE AGAINST MY THOUGHTS

My partner only says hurtful things when we are in the heat of an argument. After time has passed, they do tend to shift their position and acknowledge some of the things I was saying. We have always worked things out before. I too say hurtful things, and when I come out of the argument, I regret them. Generally, it is obvious that my partner cares about me, it's just during fights when I feel they don't. We have often figured things out after a fight and it has cleared up things that have gone unspoken for a long time. I do want to be in this relationship.

BALANCED THOUGHT

The fight really upset me, but if I let some time pass, we will figure this out and there can be some benefit from the argument. They do still love me, but we maybe need to figure out together how to communicate better and not let issues build up.

FEELINGS

Angry: 50 per cent; Frustrated: 40 per cent; Helpless: 20 per cent; Anxious: 20 per cent

By figuring out what you are actually saying to yourself (via your thoughts), you can see why you are reacting so strongly and emotionally, and why the argument was so upsetting. You went from what was probably a run-of-the-mill argument to thinking it meant something awful about your future. This is how our brains operate. Something happens and we add beliefs (e.g. if we fight, we are not meant to be together; when things are broken, they can't be fixed; people will always hurt me; I'm unlovable) into the mix, and, all of a sudden, we are reacting to something much more than an angry exchange of words about a current, run-of-the-mill situation.

EXAMPLE TWO

SITUATION

Heading back to work soon after some time off sick with stress.

FEELINGS

Anxious: 75 per cent; Embarrassed: 80 per cent: Apprehensive: 80 per cent

THOUGHTS

I shouldn't have been off for such a ridiculous reason.

I should have been able to handle this without taking time off.

Everyone else deals with stress better than I do.

Nobody else would have needed time off.

I've let my team down and left them in the lurch for a week.

My colleagues will judge me.

People will think I'm weak.

My reputation has been damaged.

Management will be doubtful about me now.

EVIDENCE FOR MY THOUGHTS

I know the environment is very stressful at the moment, but I am the only one who's been off sick. We are extremely busy and other people have had to step in and take on more work because I was not there. My manager is under a lot of pressure.

EVIDENCE AGAINST MY THOUGHTS

I have talked to two colleagues about this before and they have always been very supportive. I don't actually know what other people are thinking. If I knew someone was off because of stress, I wouldn't judge them for it. There are always people off sick and I have never had a problem helping out with their work to get things done. Having anxiety or depression is seen much less as a weakness these days: there is much more awareness and understanding. My manager has been fully supportive any time I have talked with them about this.

BALANCED THOUGHT

I do wish I was able to deal with this kind of stress better, but it was just too much this time. It's clear that those I have talked to are concerned and very supportive. I do not know what those whom I have not talked to think one way or the other, but most people these days recognise the difficulty of a mental-health issue. I am of more use back in the office when I'm feeling well and healthy.

FEELINGS

Anxious: 40 per cent; Embarrassed: 50 per cent: Apprehensive: 50 per cent

For the initial 'Thoughts' section, take as much time as you can. Really try to draw out what you are thinking and write everything down. This process is very useful, as it will slow down your thoughts because you can only write so fast. It will also get all the thoughts out of your head and can give you access to thoughts you didn't even know you were having.

If we look at the thoughts in Example Two on the previous page, we can see that, if they were to follow some of them to their most obvious conclusions, it wouldn't be long before that person would be worrying about their current job, and perhaps even their ability to hold down jobs in the future.

This may seem like a stretch, but this is the sort of place our minds can go when left to their own devices. This is why the process of writing down our thoughts can be so important, and why we sometimes need to take our thoughts out of the fog and know exactly what we are saying to ourselves.

When you start to use this method to examine your thoughts, it can be difficult to come up with evidence against your negative thoughts - especially if you are used to being hard on yourself. In the early stages, it can be very helpful to look at the first four elements in the Thought Record list, and take a step back for a moment. Then bring to mind someone you really care about, someone you'd hate to see hurt, and who you'd help out if you could. Now, imagine they have come to you with the thoughts on that page. What would you say to them? Would you tell them to get over themselves and stop being so stupid or would you have some empathy and understanding? If we can turn just 5 per cent of the concern we would have for others back to ourselves, it would be a great start. What have we got to lose?

Separating ourselves from our thoughts

We are not our thoughts.

This must be one of the biggest life lessons I have ever learned. Developing the ability to separate myself from my thoughts was perhaps the most important step I took towards really being able to manage my anxiety, as opposed to constantly firefighting and papering over the cracks. I have also witnessed this as being one of the most beneficial tools I can pass on to others.

Because my thoughts came from me, I always presumed that they were really important and completely represented who I was and what I believed. Anything my brain said to me, I took as fact. So, when it said I was weird, I believed it. When it warned of danger, I retreated. When it told me that others were not interested in what I had to say, I decided to keep quiet. And when it hit me with a horrible, intrusive thought, I believed there was something wrong with my moral compass and that I would have to monitor myself closely, otherwise I might act out those thoughts.

But the truth is, we are not our thoughts. We may be with them every moment of the day, but how much do they reflect on us?

Yes, you may sit down and decide you are going to think, for example, about the pros and cons of leaving your current job, and your mind will go to work as directed. But what about that nineties song that popped into your head earlier in the day? The one you hate, but now can't stop humming. Where did that come from? Did you summon it, decide it would be nice to hear it – or did your mind just throw it up out of nowhere?

It's hardly surprising that we pay so much attention to our anxious thoughts. As I said in Chapter 2, there was a time in our long-distant past when our ancestors would likely have ended up being killed by a predator if they didn't heed the fearful messages from their brains. We don't, of course, face those dangers now, but our brains are still wired to look out for and highlight things that are potentially dangerous.

In the work we are doing in this book, our aim is to make some of the things we worry about all the time less relevant to our brains, and we can only do this through monitoring and moderating our reactions to our thoughts.

In Chapter 4 (Anxiety Toolbox I), we looked at imagining the brain as a puppy. We feed it and look after it, so it loves us and wants to protect us. If we jump nervously when the doorbell rings, the puppy learns to bark every time someone comes to the door in an effort to keep us safe. The way we interact with our brains can be similar. If we react to a thought in a manner that confirms the danger, then, in an attempt to protect us, our brains retain that thought as important and replay it when necessary.

In Acceptance and Commitment Therapy (ACT), there is a very useful technique called 'thought defusion'. This concept rests on the recognition that, in the normal run of things, we are fused or bonded with our worrisome thoughts. We engage with them and they bind us to them. As we saw on page 95, there are thoughts we need to bring to the light and those we should treat differently.

It might not feel like it at times but, no matter what happens, we have a choice about what we do in any given situation. Victor Frankl, the renowned Austrian psychiatrist and psychotherapist, has written very powerfully about having the freedom to choose. Frankl realised this ultimate and most liberating of truths when he was a prisoner in a Nazi concentration camp during the Second World War – that even in a situation of utter powerlessness, he still had a choice in the way he responded to his circumstances.

When you are hit with a worrisome thought, you have a choice. What you have tended to do up until now is get caught up in a fight in your head, either trying to push the thought away or using rationality to defeat it. But what if the very thing you do to try and combat the worry is keeping the thoughts alive and thriving? While it's unlikely that the thoughts will go away completely, it is the fight that keeps them loud and prominent.

We may have thousands of thoughts a day, but if we were asked in the evening to recount some of them, we would probably recall just about three or four of the most worrisome ones. The other multiple-thousands of thoughts are forgotten in almost the same instant they pop up in our heads, because we do not pay them any attention or attach importance to them.

So, if we are hit with a bunch of 'what if' thoughts on a Sunday before a busy week in work, we have a choice about how we react. We can get caught up with the thoughts and have them hang around for the entire evening (which is probably our habitual pattern) or we can try and *defuse* from them. Let's look at some of the ways we can do this.

Personify the brain

A great way to distance yourself from your thoughts is to personify your brain. If you can see your brain as, for example, the boisterous but good-natured puppy mentioned on page 108 or some well-meaning but actually really unhelpful friend, you can begin to defuse yourself from the thoughts it sends you. Your brain is desperately trying to help you, but doesn't really know what is best for you. It often just throws out random thoughts and then looks to you for guidance on what to do next. If you don't react, it simply moves on. But when it sees a strong emotional response, it just keeps the thoughts coming.

It can often feel as if your mind sees fire and reaches for the petrol. If, observing this, we begin thinking, *Why do I keep doing this to myself?*, it can just add to our pain. If we can see our brains as an over-zealous friend who really wants to protect us, but is a little misguided or as a hyperactive puppy that loves us but often gets out of control, it can take the sting out of our thoughts.

So, name your brain. Something friendly – it's not a monster. For some reason, I always used Damien. I imagined him as a small, frightened boy who was constantly telling me not to do things because he wanted me to stay safe. I would be quite imaginative in my interactions with him, doing things like ruffling his hair and telling him, 'I've got this', or scooping him up and putting him on my shoulders, while saying something reassuring: 'Come on, Damien, we're going to a meeting. It'll be grand.' I had a lot of compassion for Damien – he was so small and often scared – but the more I was able to do the things he didn't want me to do, the more he saw that those things weren't as scary as he thought, and the more he was able to relax.

It got to the stage where I could keep Damien calm before he even got worked up and clamoured for my attention. I'd leave him playing with his toy trucks at home before I headed to work. If he started to get anxious, I'd invite him to come along and tell him to bring the thoughts with him, since they were not going to go away. The main point was, I was no longer going to get caught up with those thoughts and Damien's worries. They were both part of my life, but they could no longer dictate that I should stop whatever it was I was about to do.

This may sound a little off the wall, but being able to personify your brain in this way means that you can get a bit of distance from your thoughts and treat them with a little less importance. It can give you a sense of perspective that you cannot have when you are immersed in a thought pattern that is all-consuming and hard to shake off. I no longer need to use the label Damien, as I am practised enough to disengage from my thoughts without recourse to the strong imagery I once used.

Some thoughts still blindside me and I am often shocked at how sneaky and manipulative my brain can be, but when I catch what is happening, I can stop the engagement and shift my attention onto something of greater value to me.

Whatever way you want to do it, the idea is that any time your brain hits you with a 'worry thought', you simply have to acknowledge it and then push on with what you were doing. It doesn't matter how you do this. If you worry unduly about being found out at work, acknowledge the thought – 'Oh yeah, I'm a fraud. Cheers, Brain. Anyway, I have to finish this . . . ' – and then continue with what you were doing beforehand.

A quick heads-up. Your brain is used to you reacting to specific thoughts in a certain way. If you now indicate that you are no longer too concerned when one of the old familiar worrisome thoughts hits us, your brain will do a double-take: 'Eh? Hang on, we've been worrying about this for years – what do you mean, it's no longer dangerous?' So, initially, the thoughts may become louder or more persistent, but don't let this put you off. It will take time for your brain to come on board and lower the threat level usually associated with a particular thought, but, with practice and persistence, it will see that this is not just a one-off or a trick.

Name the thoughts

We have countless thoughts and can probably group our most worrisome ones into themes. If it's the persistent Sunday evening blues or the 'what if's' about the project we're on, we can categorise these, 'work worry'. If it's the repeated fear of our partner leaving, even though the relationship is good, we can call this, 'abandonment worry'. This just gives us a way to snap out of our heads when we catch ourselves drifting off into unhelpful thought patterns.

It's like when someone is telling you a story on 1 April, and, initially, you are getting sucked in by it all. The minute you realise what is going on – 'Ah, April Fool's, of course' – the power of the other person's story is gone. You can do something similar when you find yourself being caught up in one of your brain's familiar worrisome themes. Your brain may not back off in the same way as the April Fool's storyteller, but, when you figure out what is going on, you can simply choose not to engage.

Bore the worry away

Another thought defusion technique is to repeat a persistent 'worry thought' fifty times. Contrary to engaging with it, this practice serves to render the thought meaningless. If we have a fully-formed worrisome thought, we should try to break down the form it takes to one word. So, if we are at work, and we have the anxious thought that we will make a mistake on the task we are doing and get in trouble, we can sum that up with the one-word theme, 'trouble'. In fact, try and do this now as an experiment – say the word 'trouble' out loud fifty times . . .

By the time you get to the tenth time, you'll find that the word begins to lose all meaning. It gets harder to say, as you become more conscious of how your mouth moves rather than the sense of what you are saying – it's a weird sensation, and not something we normally focus on. Again, this is breaking the direct link the thoughts have to our emotions. We are looking to take away the power of the thought by blunting its piercing sting and the force of its meaning.

Mock the worry away

I know worry isn't fun, but the lighter we can keep things, the better. Again, if you can get to a place where you can see your brain as really trying to help, but not knowing how, it's easier to not get so caught up in what it tells you. If you know it is not actually trying to work against you, you can throw an arm around it and say something reassuring like, 'I know, I know – just relax.'

In his brilliant book, *The Happiness Trap*, the world-renowned ACT trainer Dr Russ Harris also asserts that, rather than challenging difficult thoughts, defusion is very often the most productive way forward.

Harris proposes that a very effective way of doing this is to put your thoughts to music, even suggesting the universally known song 'Happy Birthday To You' as a tune to use. So, take the same work worry thought from above, in its extended form – which will be something like: 'I'm going to mess up and get in trouble.' Now, start singing in your head the 'lyrics' of that thought to the tune of 'Happy Birthday':

I'm going to mess up and get in trouble,
I'm going to mess up and get in trouble,
I'm going to mess up and get in trooooooooooooouble
I'm going to mess up and get in trouble!

Here, you are letting your brain know you do not see the danger that it does. You are showing it that the worrisome thoughts about the situation do not deserve your time or emotion – they're just not relevant to what's going on right now.

Whatever you feel works best in helping you to separate from your thoughts, it is crucially important to begin the process and think about how you can build some of these techniques into your daily life. It is a process, so it will take you time to understand what strategies work best for you, and decide what tweaks are needed to make them your own. Going forward, even when you are on the plateau, you will need to remain vigilant and keep on top of things, so that you can build towards the next spike of progress on your way to mastery.

'Future Stew' will know what to do

One thing that has helped me tremendously when dealing with uncertainty in my life has been learning to trust my future self, who I nicknamed 'Future Stew'. Constant, anticipatory anxiety was always a huge issue for me. I would spend long periods of time worrying how an event would unfold (usually a mundane work-day situation), and then, an hour into the day I dreaded, everything would be fine. My worry would always tell me I couldn't do things, but those things kept getting done anyway. It got to a stage where there was a real, consistent disconnect between my predictions of the future and how that future actually played out.

The more I looked at the reality of these situations, the more I learned to trust Future Stew, because I could see that he never let me down. He found things difficult, undoubtedly, and had to learn from many mistakes, but he was able to cope. I trusted that guy more than I trusted myself! If I looked back on any event, Future Stew always managed much better than I thought he would – and yet I always doubted him. It was ridiculous. Over time, I learned to hand things over to him, safe in the knowledge that he would sort it out, which meant I could stop worrying about it and just go to sleep. I managed to get to the point where it wasn't a case of just hoping that things would work out: I actively cultivated a genuine trust in the future version of me.

So much of our worry is tied up with overestimating the threat and underestimating our ability to cope – but if we were to stand back and look at things objectively, we will see that we've always coped. Even if we could have done better or might have thought at the time that we didn't cope, we always at least survived and learned a valuable lesson. So many of my clients have the same kind of difficulty with future worry – and yet when we examine their pasts, they have dealt with loss of parents, jobs and relationships, serious health issues, huge financial difficulties, and whatever else life has thrown their way. When they got to the actual feared event, they had somehow found a way to cope.

The future version of yourself does not have to deal with worry. It doesn't have to deal with all the 'what if' thoughts, worst-case scenarios or foggy thinking. It has to deal with the actual situation when it presents itself, and it always gets through that. The Future You gets to face a real event, not a hundred imagined ones.

And when a real event unfolds, it goes into action mode and worry often disappears. There can be fear, for sure, but when we are in the moment, we are fully capable, we have something tangible to deal with and we almost always come through OK – and even if we don't think we have, we will survive in any case.

In this strategy of handing over a situation to our future selves, there is again an element of thought defusion, where we will not allow ourselves to engage. We just acknowledge the thought and move on: 'Thanks for that, Brain. I'm not sure how we're going to do this either, but Future Stew will figure it out. Now, I have to go to work and get on with my day.'

Chapter 7

Anxiety in the Workplace – Part One

If we are prone to anxiety, there are few areas of our lives where it does not play its part, large or small. Perhaps where it can affect us most is in our working lives, where so much is out of our hands, and where stress, deadlines and evaluation are part and parcel of the daily routine. This is often a place where we show very little of ourselves at the best of times. For many people, it is certainly not a place where we allow ourselves to appear anxious or nervous.

As we have seen in Chapters 3 and 5, if we are worriers, intrusive thoughts about future events can be all-consuming, and, at the heart of this, is a deep-seated need for control and certainty. In a busy working environment, however, certainty can be in short supply. Much of what we have to deal with in our day-to-day working life is complex, and certainly not always clear-cut and predictable. We cannot always foresee how a future project will go, who we will have to work with or what pressure will be involved. We cannot always anticipate all the obstacles we may encounter or how our manager, colleagues or clients will react.

When we begin to progress at work and things get busier, our anxieties may intensify and our habitual methods of regulating our mood may become less effective. If we get to the stage where our coping reservoir is almost full before we even realise the water level of our anxiety is on the rise (see Chapter 2), we may soon begin to find that the smallest things have become difficult to handle. We start to doubt ourselves and our ability to cope. Every interaction with our boss is fraught with fear and trepidation as we presume we are going to be found out. Before we know it, we are suddenly feeling overwhelmed and unsure of what the hell just happened.

To ensure we do not get to this place, it is crucial to start becoming more aware of, and in turn tackling, the issues that are causing us most difficulty in the workplace. In this chapter, as well as considering how to tackle the anxiety and worry which can directly undermine our everyday, ongoing performance at work, we will look at some of the most common tendencies of the anxious personality – such as perfectionism and Impostor Syndrome. We will see how these traits and tendencies can play out at work and, most crucially, explore how we can go about challenging and countering them to minimise their negative effects in our professional lives, and make our dealings at work simpler, more straightforward and, above all, more fulfilling.

In Chapter 8, we will look at what happens when we get a promotion and at the new set of challenges that comes with managing others and consider how to deal with them and with difficult people in general. We'll finish off with a look at one of the most problematic areas at work for those suffering with social anxiety – the work meeting – and consider some useful strategies you can put into practice in such situations. The emphasis throughout will be on providing practical steps and tools, which I and my clients have found most helpful in each area.

Getting your anxiety under control and into a manageable state going forward needs to be the goal. It is hard enough to keep on top of your work, deal with the complexities of the modern workplace and have one eye on your career in the longer term, without the constant pain and mental noise of unrestricted worry. If you can learn to manage anxiety as early in your working life as possible, you will feel the positive effects in terms of the nature and quality of the work you do, how you progress in your chosen career, whether you are paid what you deserve, and just how far you can go if you keep pushing beyond the boundaries of your comfort zone.

So, before you look around in five years' time and see that all your peers have moved on, that a new group of young and hungry employees are coming through, and that you have not progressed or upskilled, it is the time to start tackling the anxiety that is stalling your career and keeping you shackled to the familiar and undemanding. If you start addressing your fears, they may even turn out not to be as scary as you think. There is only one way to find out.

The hidden cost of anxiety: how worry steals our attention and concentration

Work is definitely one place where we need to be able to concentrate, take in information and decide on the best course of action with a clear head. There are so many ways in which anxious thoughts can take us out of the present moment and leave us knocking around in our own heads. If we are prone to worry, it's not just that we resort to worry when we are stressed or under pressure, it's that we tend to worry even when things are going fine.

As we saw in Chapter 3, worriers have no more thoughts than anyone else. The issue is that they generally tend towards negative thoughts, get much more involved with them and pay them much more attention so that they experience them as loud and disruptive. And if we cannot tolerate feeling anxious, we may look for comfort and escape, which only saps our attention and ability to focus even further.

We will sometimes conclude that we just have a short attention span, are absentminded or simply cannot focus – or even that we are actually just lazy – such is our inability to recognise the distracting power of our anxiety. This can have a huge effect on our productivity and our interactions with other people at work.

Constant task switching

One of the ways anxiety can seriously hamper our levels of efficiency is that it can result in a tendency to flit constantly from one task to another in our rush to get everything done. If, for example, we have four tasks to complete in a day, worrying we won't get them all done may cause us to switch rapidly between the four, without getting much traction on any of them. The more we fret about not getting anything done, the less able we will be to settle on one job and just churn through it until we have it under control. The less traction we get, the more distracted and anxious we become – and so the cycle continues.

During times like this, it can be helpful to practise some of the thought separation techniques from Chapter 6 (Anxiety Toolbox II), and make ourselves stay focused on one task.

In my own case, when I worked in IT, I used to feel that I was never good with tight deadlines and the challenge of having to complete lots of tasks within a short space of time. The uncertainty around whether or not I'd manage to hit the deadline always caused my brain to ramp up the worry thoughts. When I figured out that what my brain actually needed and what I thought it was looking for were two different things, I was able to quieten the worry. I was operating under the mistaken assumption that what I craved was a comforting response to all the 'what if' questions – when, in fact, what my brain really needed was simply to see me making progress. When I engaged less with the thoughts and put in some productive time on one task, my brain began to calm down.

Most often, the problem is not that the job in hand is beyond our usual remit or our competence, but rather that we will just not allow ourselves to get to it. We simply need to put everything else aside and truly focus. In this context, a phrase from my time working in tech companies always comes to mind: 'Stop starting and start finishing!' It's much more productive to stay on one task until it is finished rather than jumping constantly from one thing to another.

Another helpful strategy when we are finding it hard to maintain focus is to try working in short, twenty-five-minute bursts. Even those of us who don't have to contend with anxiety can find it hard to concentrate for extended periods. Removing the expectation that we should be able to focus for an hour – let alone hours – at a time can really help us maximise productivity during these shorter bursts of activity. After a short break of five minutes or so, we then return to the task for another twenty-five-minute stint. It is always surprising how much you can get done in a short, focused period of time.

In Chapter 9 (Anxiety Toolbox III), we will be looking at some mindfulness techniques that can come in very useful when we have a lot of tasks to complete within a short time, but find that our thoughts are scattered. At the core of the discipline of mindfulness is the practice of regularly returning to the present moment each time our mind begins to wander and the rabbit-hole of worry beckons. In this context, we consciously bring our focus to the task at hand and then, when we feel ourselves inevitably drift away with our thoughts, we gently bring ourselves back to the present, to our physical environment and to the task we are engaged in.

Sometimes, we feel we cannot start something because we only have a small window of time and it's a major piece of work. In this instance, try not to listen to your brain when it tells you that there isn't enough time to do something on it. Short bursts of work in small increments can really get us moving through a task, rather than us feeling we need to spend a long time with something to be productive. In this scenario, it's important to break the work up into smaller sections or tasks, so we can actually complete some parts of a bigger job. As we observe ourselves getting started and getting through work, our brain will lower the threat level and our anxiety will diminish accordingly.

Funnily enough, as I am writing this very section, my mind is constantly reminding me how much work I have to do to finish this book! This kind of thinking is something I have always struggled with when it comes to tackling major, long-term projects. I'll find my brain firing off a series of questions and conundrums. *What about the other chapters? Should I get some of them done first? Will I have enough time to get everything finished? Will it be good enough?* Noise, noise, noise!

If I allow myself to get caught up in these thoughts, they will become louder and more persistent, since I have acknowledged the danger they're trying to alert me to. At this stage in my life and career, I am generally able to keep them at bay, by not engaging and simply concentrating on what I am doing – but I'm aware that they are always there, looking for attention, waiting in the wings for the moment when I'll give in and finally listen to them! I've learned to treat them like that eager puppy, by saying something like: 'Not now, Worry Thoughts – I have a book to write. Join me if you must, but we're doing this at the moment.'

Avoidance and procrastination

As I've said previously, there is nothing that lowers anxiety about a task more quickly than the feeling that we are getting through it. Equally, however, if we feel we can't start something or are getting nowhere, excessive worrying can affect our ability to tackle the job head-on. If we fear a piece of work is too large or difficult, we may put off starting it. This can become the slippery slope of procrastination, where we will find a way to distract ourselves from the task at hand. Alternatively, we might start another easier, lower priority job to try to make ourselves feel like we are still being productive.

Our priority work, however, remains untouched – and now we have even less time. We may find ourselves thinking that this task is too difficult and begin doubting our ability to complete it. We may stray even further down the rabbit-hole of worry, fretting about what will happen when we inevitably mess up the whole thing and everyone is angry with us.

As we have seen in Chapter 3, intrusive thoughts about future events can be all-consuming. As our thoughts become intolerable, our concentration is shot to pieces and so we might pick up our phone and start looking at social media for a sense of momentary relief. For a while, it works and we distract ourselves from our thoughts, but as soon as we put down the phone, we know that the problem is still there.

This method is about learning to trust our own capacity to understand what needs to be done *and* our ability to get it finished. Our anxiety is making us see the threat as insurmountable and our ability to cope as insufficient. It's our dread of uncertainty that is at play here again. When we start a task, we may not know what we need to do but surely we trust ourselves to figure it out? We may not have done this task before, but surely we have confidence that all the skills and experience we already have will help us? Once again, we must learn to become more accepting that uncertainty is a natural part of life and that we cannot avoid it in work, just as we can't in any other context.

In this kind of situation, a quick Thought Record (Chapter 6, Anxiety Toolbox II) can be very helpful in terms of settling your nerves. It can be great if we get to the stage where we can do this in our heads. As I pointed out in Chapter 6, the more Thought Records we do on paper, the more practised we will become at them and the more able we will be to run through this technique mentally and in as close to real time as possible.

Firstly, instead of desperately trying to push the thoughts away, try to work out what you are saying to yourself. Can you look back on the evidence of other jobs you have done? This one is no different. Have there been previous jobs where you didn't know what to do initially, but, when you gave yourself the time, you were able to figure it out? Are there any gaps in your knowledge or is there any information needed that you could ask a colleague about? Can you allow yourself to ask questions without feeling stupid or that you 'should' already know the answer? If one of your colleagues was just starting something and wanted to talk it over, would you immediately think they were not good at their job or would you just see it as a normal part of the process and be more than willing to help?

This may be a time when you need to hand over the problem to your future self. As we discovered in Chapter 3 (Worry) and in Chapter 6 (Anxiety Toolbox II), your future self will handle any situation when it arises to the best of its ability. It is the present version of you that has to deal with the doom-laden fantasy of all the 'what if's'. The worst thing you can do is avoid starting a task or, if it's required, not reach out for some guidance on where you might go with this. If either of these options seems too difficult, have a think about how the conversation would go if you just left things until the deadline and had to explain why you haven't finished the assignment!

The key principle here is that when we allow ourselves to start a task and get our teeth into it, it begins to get more manageable. Starting is half the battle. If we can quieten the voice that is telling us we are not good enough, and use the evidence of previous jobs we have got through as reassurance that we have what it takes to handle something, then we are well on our way. There is nothing like showing ourselves we can cope to allay anxiety.

Worry and interactions with others at work

Just as anxiety negatively affects our productivity, it can also have a major impact on our focus and concentration in our interactions with others at work. When we are talking to a colleague or manager, and they are giving us information on an upcoming task or project, worrisome thoughts can play havoc with our ability to take in what we are being told. We might hear the first part and then lose ourselves in imagining the worst-case scenarios or trying to solve problems that do not yet exist. All the while, we have mentally checked out of the conversation and will potentially miss further crucial information, such as possible solutions, useful ideas or suggestions about people who may be able to help.

It is important to be aware that this is how anxiety can affect us in conversation. Can we stay focused on the person we are talking to and what they are saying, rather than running off immediately with our own thoughts? We have to be conscious of this in order to tackle it. It may take much trial and error in order to make real progress here. We can start off by simply noticing when we start to head off into our thoughts and then bring ourselves back into the conversation each time, without harshly judging the fact we wandered. Harsh judgement never helps.

We need to allow ourselves to fail and slowly get better

because, if this is a problem, it can be a difficult one to work through. Again, this is much the same process that is used to bring ourselves back into the present moment in mindfulness, which will be outlined in Chapter 9 (Anxiety Toolbox III).

In order to stay focused and take in important information, we can repeat back to the other person a brief summary of what they have just said, which also clarifies things for both parties. If we leave a conversation feeling that we have missed some important parts, we need to go easy on ourselves and acknowledge that this is a difficult problem to overcome. We need to bear in mind that we can always go back to the source of the information for further clarification.

Social anxiety at work

As well as our anxieties about taking in the details of and being able to handle the work assigned to us by others, social anxiety - fear of embarrassment or judgement from others - can hamper our interactions with colleagues hugely and affect how well we are able to do our job on a daily basis. When we are constantly worried about what people think of us, it can affect how we operate and take our attention away from the environment around us, as we focus inwards on how we feel, how we are being viewed and what we might say.

This can play havoc in meetings. If our main focus is on the possibility of being asked a question and how we might respond or how we might look if we don't know the answer, we are very likely not concentrating on what is actually being said. We may believe our answers have to be of the highest standard, otherwise we will be judged harshly, which means that, when put on the spot, it is very hard to come up with a spontaneous answer that meets these expectations.

This type of internal focus can actually make us appear spaced out or uninterested. If we are talking to a colleague or manager, instead of listening to what they are saying, our main concern is about saying the right thing or making a good impression. This, in turn, may leave us with our mind going blank when we need to respond. Much of the work that is needed here is covered in Chapter 5 (Socially Anxious), which I would advise going back over when looking at handling interactions with colleagues. Some positive experimentation, as outlined in Chapter 5, may be very useful here.

Another key part of getting better is to not destroy yourself in the post-mortem. If you come away from an exchange with a boss or colleague, feeling that it could have gone better, can you at least go easy on yourself and not presume it was the worst thing that could have happened and that everyone now thinks you're an idiot?

We will also be looking in more detail at strategies for handling important work meetings in Chapter 8 (Anxiety in the Workplace – Part Two).

The anxious personality

Let's take a look at some personality traits and deep-seated beliefs that are most common in worriers and which can have a negative impact on our working life in much more general, long-term ways. In considering these, we'll also be exploring some techniques and strategies for overcoming some of the difficulties associated with these traits, and how we can avoid making our working environment more stressful than it needs to be.

Impostor Syndrome

Many of us who are anxious struggle with a fear of being found out, which is known as the 'Impostor Syndrome'. This is a recognised psychological pattern, whereby someone constantly doubts their accomplishments and has a persistent, internalised fear of being exposed as a 'fraud'.

Here's how Impostor Syndrome works.

Everything we have achieved in our lives, and every position we ever have held in our careers, can be explained away by sheer luck, good timing, the kindness of others or even the intervention of a divine power. Everyone else out there is so much better than we are, in every sense – more deserving, more accomplished and more confident. We are convinced that the people who have hired us have been duped, taken in, had the wool pulled over their eyes. We are also absolutely certain that when we are finally – and inevitably – found out, we will be utterly humiliated, and that, before we are escorted from the premises, we will also have to suffer the guilt of looking our boss in the eye, as they reel at our deception. 'And to think I trusted and believed in you,' they might say with a disappointed shake of the head, as we are led away.

OK, so maybe I've gone a bit too far – but you get the picture!

Ultimately, we feel fraudulent and that it is only a matter of time before we are exposed as exactly that. And in our minds, what is worse than exposure, public humiliation and embarrassment? Other than, perhaps, death, this kind of exposure is one of our greatest fears as humans.

Impostor Syndrome plays havoc in our working lives. It makes downtime impossible to be comfortable with or enjoy, as we always feel people are looking over our shoulder, wondering what value we are bringing.

Constantly doubting your abilities makes it hard to have a good working relationship with your boss, and, if you do manage that, you are haunted that the inevitable sense of betrayal this individual will feel when you let them down will be too much for you to handle. How can you push yourself forward and progress in your career if you believe everything about you is a lie?

While all sorts of people are affected by Impostor Syndrome, it is particularly prominent in people who struggle with social anxiety or general anxiety. If we are already a worrier and constantly preoccupied with what others think of us, this fear of exposure is likely to be part of our daily mindset at work.

It's time to confront this fear, and get our Impostor Syndrome under control and out of our lives. Acknowledge it, challenge it – then let it go.

Here are some guidelines to help you manage this process.

Acknowledge that this is how you are feeling and that Impostor Syndrome is a very common thing – it's something that a lot of people struggle with, including many successful people. This way, you can begin to normalise these feelings and stop seeing yourself as 'different' or 'not normal'. Acknowledge that Impostor Syndrome is a common human experience and that a lot of people suffer from it, but that it is not real.

Anxiety thrives on vagueness. Walking around with an undefined, anxious feeling or a vague sense of unease, is the perfect environment for an anxious mind to go into overdrive. You need to start looking at the actual facts, but to remove yourself from the picture as you do so (since you are an expert at dismissing positive evidence about yourself).

You can achieve this by imagining you are talking to a friend who is struggling with Impostor Syndrome. How have you actually been doing over the past few months or years? What has your manager said about you? How have appraisals gone? What have you been trusted with? How are you seen by your peers? What have you accomplished?

Try to do this objectively, and not through the 'I'm rubbish' filter. Sometimes, talking about yourself in the third person, even using a different name, can help. 'Janet/Peter has actually been doing pretty well recently . . .'

Keep finding things you do well, and reasons for which you may be valued. Keep a diary, if needed, or a weekly achievements sheet because if you are prone to worry, you will tend to focus on your weaknesses and lose sight of or overlook your strengths. As you do this work, you need to be always conscious of the power of Impostor Syndrome – 'I am struggling with feelings of fraudulence, therefore, I will always doubt my own abilities.' Keep pushing through any resistance, finding things you do well and reasons colleagues may value you (whether these qualities have explicitly been acknowledged by others or are things we do or qualities that we would value in a workmate).

Continuing this evidence-gathering approach, you can now ask yourself if it's possible that it is you who are underestimating your own talents, and if those who hired you, and have kept you on, might have a more objective view of your strengths and abilities? Are you saying that it's obvious that you are fooling everyone and that so many intelligent people have been hoodwinked and are blind to your ineptitude? Maybe, just maybe, you need to trust the judgement of those above and around you on this one. Perhaps, at this moment in time, *you* are the one whose judgement is skewed.

A key feature of Impostor Syndrome is that, as well as constantly underestimating our own strengths, we continually overplay the talents of others. We usually pick the one skill or personality trait that a colleague has that we do not, meaning we are unfairly judging ourselves against someone else's 'super power'. So, it is crucially important that we stop comparing ourselves to others. We are unable to be objective when we are in the Impostor Syndrome mindset and comparison invariably goes badly for us. Until we are able to acknowledge our own strengths and abilities more accurately, we need to just stop.

We have to allow ourselves to make mistakes and to learn from them. We need to afford ourselves the right to not know and the option of coming back to someone later. What often feeds into Impostor Syndrome is an inability, or unwillingness, to see everything as a learning process. There are very few jobs any more where you master one skill or one approach and that's it for the next forty years! If we are to have a full and varied career, we will always be living on the edge of our comfort zone. We will never be definitive experts at everything – as soon as we approach the mark, we will be challenged in some other way by being given a new role or being moved to a new job. This has to happen if we are to progress and grow.

We need to become more comfortable in this space where we do not know everything, and challenging Impostor Syndrome is a huge part of this process. If we are constantly telling ourselves we are not good enough for the job, any mistake or gap in our knowledge will be seen by us as the proof of this. Working to diminish these feelings will enable us to be more comfortable with the level we are at. We may also need to take stock of the role perfectionism plays in this sense of never feeling good enough (we'll be looking at this in the next section).

As with some of the other anxious thought patterns we've looked at, when we have thoroughly addressed

Impostor Syndrome and the feelings around it, through
challenge, balance and fair analysis, we need to leave
it be. We cannot start challenging it over and over each
time it crops up, as this will only confirm to our brain the
sense of danger, thereby keeping the thoughts strong.
We should try to simply be aware when it is at play and
then, using the thought defusion tools from Chapter 6
(Anxiety Toolbox II), acknowledge it and go about our
business. We can call it out, 'Ah, here's the old Impostor
Syndrome. I've to go to a meeting, Brain, so come on,
bring on the thoughts if you want to – but then, let's go.'
In this way, we are telling our brain that we know it's
worried, but that we do not see the same level of threat
here as it does.

Perfectionism

Perfectionism and anxiety are not a good mix.

If we consistently hold ourselves to account and
continually push ourselves to reach our goals and
improve our situation, then fantastic. If, however, we
insist on unattainably high standards in every little
thing we do, where simply meeting the bar we have set
is the minimum we expect of ourselves and falling in
any way short throws us into an anxiety tailspin, then
this can become problematic.

This way of operating plagued much of my corporate
working life. There was one stage, early in my IT career,
where I'd be asked to carry out simple estimates on
prospective small jobs coming to the team I was working
in. What was needed was not much more than a finger-

in-the-air guesstimate, backed by a bit of knowledge of the general work involved. These estimates should have been easy enough to do, but I agonised over each one for far longer than the task warranted. I would generate spreadsheets with detailed breakdowns, constantly terrified that if I underestimated, the job would be bigger than we had planned, but that if I overestimated, I would look stupid and possibly even lose us the job unnecessarily. I never told anyone just how much time I'd have to spend on all this, and my manager loved the format of the estimates I prepared – so I quickly became the go-to person on the team for this task! Each time another estimate was needed from me, my other work suffered greatly and my anxiety levels went through the roof because my perfectionism did not care about mitigating circumstances. All my work had to meet a certain, very high standard, regardless of its actual importance.

How perfectionism affects our work

Perfectionism and our own unrelenting standards can be a curse in our professional lives. They can of course ensure that we generally put out quality work, however, such perfectionism can often also mean that every job we have to do becomes ten times more intimidating, ten times longer and ten times more anxiety-inducing, as we grapple with the fear of not meeting our own standards. These standards are applied to big and small tasks alike, regardless of their actual importance.

An email of little consequence can take fifteen minutes

to complete, as we write and rewrite it, checking for any kind of inadequacy that could be read into our words. *Might anyone on the CC-list possibly be offended by what I've said here? Should I say it another way instead?* And so we can find ourselves caught up in small, meaningless tasks for so long that there's now less time for the bigger, more important stuff that has yet to be done – but which must still be done perfectly.

The tasks we work on have to be checked and double-checked before we can show them to anyone – and even then, self-doubt can continue to gnaw at us. As you can imagine, if we operate like this for any length of time, the unfinished tasks rapidly mount up, and next thing we know, our work–life balance is heavily skewed towards work.

Perfectionism can also stop us from reaching out for help – firstly, because we cannot be seen to be lacking, but also because maybe we only trust our own way of doing things and don't trust others not to make a mistake. We believe they may not have our standards, that they will not check as thoroughly or cover every angle the way we would. If our name is to be on a piece of work, it has to be completely error-free, and so even when we allow ourselves to get help, it can add time to the task, since now we have to check the other person's work as well as our own.

We may believe that we have to work all the time, so as not to appear lazy, or that we must be faultless, so others cannot see the person that we fear we are. This fear can play out as Impostor Syndrome, which we have discussed on pages 131-6, where we believe that we will be found out as frauds and so we have to keep up the charade with perfect work.

The need to be perfect at all times and in all things in work can play out in other ways too. When I deal with perfectionism-related anxiety with my clients, I find it tends to go one of two ways. On the one hand, it can keep us feeling as though we've convinced everyone around us that we're a really solid person (but this can take an enormous toll, as we have said). Conversely, perfectionism can be such a tyrannical monster that it can make us feel that it is easier to just not try at all. Why attempt to satisfy that which cannot be satisfied? And so the need to be perfect can keep us stuck and unable to start a new project because it is so difficult to reach our own impossibly high bar. Not trying becomes infinitely better than trying and failing, especially because most perfectionists cannot tolerate the possibility of making mistakes.

Why do we do this to ourselves?

Well, one reason is that we presume the world is judging us as harshly as we are judging ourselves. Everyone else is as critical, impatient and unforgiving as we are with ourselves. If we can see a mistake we have made or something we could have done better, well, we can be sure that everyone else has spotted it too. And guess what? They feel as disgusted, as appalled, as let down as we do.

Take a look at the list on the next page, and see if any of these apply to you.

1. I must do all things perfectly.

2. Mistakes are not allowed, as they will highlight my inadequacy.

3. If I try, I will most likely fail.

4. If I make a mistake, I will be rejected.

5. If I put my work out there, it is inevitable that others will think badly of me.

6. Doing well isn't good enough – I have to do better than that.

7. If I don't strive to achieve higher standards, I am a lazy and useless person.

8. My work is never as good as I want it to be.

9. I can't let anyone else do a task on my behalf in case it goes wrong.

10. I have to check over any work I do several times before I can show it to anyone.

11. There is a right way and a wrong way to do things – no in-between.

12. I prefer to either do something perfectly and to 100 per cent of my ability or not do it at all.

13. People will always judge me as harshly as I judge myself.

Becoming less vigilant

In tackling the downsides of perfectionism in our working lives, we need to try to allow ourselves to think in less black-and-white terms. Unless we are in the first week of a job, what people at work think of us does not change on a daily basis – and even in this scenario, we are generally given time to grow into a role before opinions are formed. When our colleagues and managers have got a general take on us, and if our work tends to be of a good standard, making a single mistake will not change that or cause them to do a complete turnaround on us. This can be difficult for perfectionists to believe and it is especially difficult if we have a boss who tends to sound off a lot and snap when things aren't going their way.

It is important to understand, however, that our reputation is not on the line every time we go into work. We do not need to be constantly vigilant or spend an unproductive amount of time second-guessing other people and continually trying to figure out if they think less of us for some small thing we said or did. This kind of thinking will make for a very stressful environment and a heightened level of emotional alert, which is unproductive when it comes to keeping anxiety under control.

It is worth asking ourselves if our perfectionism is a way of keeping our opinions of ourselves at bay, as much as those of other people. If we believe that we are useless, incompetent, talentless or generally a fraud in the professional environment, we may think that turning out quality work at all times will at least enable us to feel a little more neutral about ourselves and keep the real negativity at bay. Do give this some serious thought. If this is how you are operating, it would be good to bring it out of the fog so that you can begin to challenge some of the thoughts and beliefs that lie behind it.

When thinking about these issues, can we try to bring in the compassion that we would no doubt have for other people who shared with us such thoughts about themselves? What would we say to a friend who was telling us this story? Would we agree and tell them they were useless and a fraud in spite of all their achievements or would we have some counterarguments to make? Often, behind the accolades and achievements we have been so driven to notch up, we can have a very poor opinion of ourselves and very low self-worth. If this is a really entrenched problem, it would be a good exercise to get a piece of paper and pen, and write about what it means if we do not do everything perfectly. This could bring up some very interesting points for further exploration.

Behind perfectionism, there can also be the unfounded belief that the only thing that is keeping us from crumbling completely and descending into a state of chaos, in which we could not get the simplest task over the line, is the constant drive of our unrelenting standards. That if we lower our standards even just occasionally, we will all at once do everything really poorly and everyone else will suddenly see us for what we actually are. This is similar thinking to the belief that worrying about everything is the only thing keeping us focused and enables us to get things done. In reality, if we did not constantly strive to be perfect, we would still put out a level of work that would be totally adequate. It's this intolerance for less than perfect every time that is the issue here, and, as we have said above, this can end up making perfect work either impossible or so time-consuming that it affects our overall standard of work anyway.

Good enough, more often than not, is good enough

Have a think about how perfectionism is playing out for you presently in the professional realm. Does it really mean that you are productive and that your work is always of a high standard? At what cost does that high standard come? Does it leave you stuck and fearful of starting anything? Does it stop you asking others for help or mean that you only do so when things have gone too far or when it'll be really hard to turn things around?

Next, ask yourself how this might play out in your career going forward. If you cannot trust anyone to help you because you feel they don't have your standards, how will this work out if you get to a stage where you're required to manage a team? No doubt it will lead to micro-management, with you constantly looking over people's shoulders and being very critical of their work, and yet obliged to stand over it. How will those on your team react to such a style of management? We need to address this kind of thinking before we progress any further.

When you allow yourself to be less than perfect sometimes, you can lower your anxiety levels and become more productive. Being cautious of making mistakes can help you be vigilant and improve performance, but as always, it's about balance. If mistakes are utterly unacceptable, then this can keep you from making any move at all. Your beliefs about mistakes need to be challenged here. There almost certainly is an element of worst-case scenario thinking, where mistakes are shameful, will have terrible consequences, or will do damage to your reputation. Generally, this is not the case. Mistakes are to be expected as part of the human experience. We are regularly our own worst critics and others will not judge our mistakes as harshly as we judge ourselves. The truth is that often the extra work we put into insuring our work is mistake-free is unnecessary and will go unnoticed.

Other people are not always looking for an opportunity to criticise us. In fact, the reality is that most of the work we do, and the emails we send, will not come under the degree of scrutiny we fear. Can you save your perfectionism for the priority, high-exposure work? Not every small task needs to be gold-plated. Not every email you send has to be read and reread ten times. It may sound counterintuitive, especially in a professional environment, but when it comes to the everyday tasks, you may need to lower your standards. I bet all that you do will still be absolutely good enough!

Chapter 8
Anxiety in the Workplace – Part Two

Climbing the ladder

As we progress in our careers, those who suffer from anxiety may find that things tend to get harder, rather than easier. If moving up leaves us open to a lot of our fears, we can be reluctant to go for promotions or roles that require more responsibility and exposure. And yet, if the alternative is to stay safe and comfortable, never moving beyond our established boundaries or original skill set, we are consigning ourselves to a future without challenge, learning or growth. And the reality is that, in the current world of work, there are very few safe and comfortable positions that we can remain in forever.

The desire to please others and win their approval is a very common tendency in anxious personality types, and this is also undoubtedly one of the biggest sticking points when it comes to furthering our careers and moving up the ladder at work. It is very important to try to get to grips with some of the drawbacks of always putting others first and needing constant validation before we get hit with the issues moving up can throw at us.

People-pleasing: when the needs of others trump our own

Many people who have trouble with anxiety will identify to some extent with the term 'people-pleaser'. It might not feel like a great thing to have to admit about ourselves, as the term tends to have negative connotations and is often seen as something of a weakness. While, unsurprisingly, this characteristic can make us great team players, it can throw up a lot of problems when we have to look after our own interests. In salary negotiations, for example, if we are more concerned with fairness and with the other person getting what they want, rather than our own needs being met, then we are always operating from a place of weakness. And when we reach management level, as we have said, our difficulties will only be compounded.

People-pleasers will find many of the following things very challenging:

» Conflict

» Voicing a contrary opinion to a colleague, a boss or the rest of team as a whole

» Taking control of a situation

» Making difficult decisions – not just because
we risk the disapproval of colleagues, but also
because in always trying to please others, we
have lost touch with our own instincts and
wisdom about what is best

» Taking credit for their own work

» Saying 'no' to work when they already have too
much to do

» Giving an honest status report on a difficult
project

» Taking time off

» Asking for a raise

» Seeking a promotion

» Putting themselves first.

This list is by no means exhaustive, but in the context
of succeeding and progressing in the workplace, it is
self-evident that this kind of thinking will hold us back.
The need to be liked by everyone will make us conflict-
avoidant, as we worry about being seen as uncooperative,
difficult or not a team player.

When it comes to a career, a people-pleaser may not
even know what they want themselves, let alone how to
get it. One of the many negative effects of constantly

considering the wants and needs of others ahead of our own is that we never develop much of a sense of our own preferences or wishes. Even if we do have an idea of what we want, getting there can be very difficult if we never make ourselves a priority.

The constant need for external validation and acceptance also comes with the territory for people-pleasers. We feel OK when we have been told we are OK. We feed off praise and when it is absent we are left with uncertainty, which is not a place where we feel at all comfortable. In this scenario, the more the doubt creeps in, the more our brains go about undermining us.

When we find something easy, we presume it must be easy for everyone, rather than acknowledging that we have an aptitude for it. We do not value our strengths, and focus on our weaknesses to such an extent that they are all we can see about ourselves. This is something to think seriously about if you are doing, or thinking about doing, a job that involves a lot of solitary work or working from home without a lot of access to your colleagues or a manager. Being left to figure out for yourself how well you are doing, and what people think of you, is a really tricky situation for a people-pleaser.

The people-pleaser is often a boss's dream. Always there, willing to do whatever it takes, loyal to the end, and making few or no demands. We may see our peers progressing much faster than we do, as we stay in jobs with little gratification because we don't value our skills enough to apply elsewhere. But perhaps most of all, we don't want to let our boss down. After all they have done for us, how could we possibly stab them in the back by moving somewhere else? It is this unfounded fear of hurting other people's feelings that also causes so many problems for the people-pleaser. Perhaps we grew up in an environment where those around us, on whom we depended for our survival, were overly sensitive and easily hurt or angered and so we learned to feel responsible for the emotions of others. But the working environment is certainly not the place to carry forward this way of thinking.

We may believe that looking after our own interests is selfish or will be seen as selfish. We will do almost anything to be liked. Saying 'no' becomes taboo, as we take on work that is not our own and feed off the smiles and thanks of those around us. The more we do, however, the more others will lean on us, and so we take on more responsibility, but with none of the credit. Ultimately, this can lead to feelings of anger and resentment – but we have no outlet for these in the workplace, as we know we can't be universally liked whilst showing negative emotions. The more those around us scoop up the plaudits and promotions, the more we feel our achievements should be noticed, and that we shouldn't have to go around shouting about all our qualities.

Bearing all of this in mind, it stands to reason that managing others can be very tricky for the people-pleaser. If we have assertiveness problems with those who report to us, or try too hard to please everyone on our team, we can have real difficulties exerting the proper authority needed to keep the team running effectively, whilst giving everyone the confidence that we can lead them. How can we delegate when we hate to put people out or have anyone annoyed with us? How can we say 'no' to time off or holiday requests during busy periods when we are more concerned with the needs of others than our own? How can we tell someone they are not performing to a high enough standard when we cannot abide conflict?

We haven't even talked about keeping those above us happy yet. Our bosses in upper management or other parties in the business will want output: they are looking for solutions, action, progress and productivity. Their first priority isn't necessarily the wellbeing of the team or how happy everyone is.

Validation may be in very short supply as we go into firefighting mode, running from nerve-wracking meeting to nerve-wracking meeting during the busy periods of a project. What happens now if we don't have the full respect of our team or we have employees who take advantage of our easy-going nature or we routinely accept or even praise sub-par work? This is when the worry can go into overdrive and become too much to cope with, as we cannot get a rest from our thoughts and every little thing we have to deal with gets blown up in our minds into something bigger than it should be.

'The squeaky wheel gets the grease'

It is imperative that we find our voice and begin to come out of the shadows. If we look at who is getting the promotions and pay rises, they are people asking for them, making the case as to why they should be getting them and leaving their managers in no doubt that if they do not get them, they have other options. As my dear old gran used to say, 'The squeaky wheel gets the grease.' We need to manage our manager or, if we are managers ourselves, those we answer to in upper management. Let them know what we are doing and that we need recognition. We need to start squeaking!

Let's explore a few ways in which you can start to challenge unproductive people-pleasing habits.

Begin by noticing every time you sacrifice your own needs for those of others. This shouldn't be hard in that, as people-pleasers, we may be doing this constantly. The problem, however, might be that we are so used to putting our needs to the bottom of our list of priorities that we may no longer recognise what they are! We might also be reluctant to let go of the selflessness we see as an important part of who we are, and which often attracts the praise and validation from others that we most crave.

Learn to say 'no'. Start with something small. Can we push back on work that is not ours, and not let others take advantage of our kindness? In order to do this, we need to address the belief we have about what others will think if we say 'no'. We presume they will feel let down, or that they will change their opinion of us, but this very often isn't true. This is a perfect situation to work through with a Thought Record from Chapter 6 (Anxiety Toolbox II).

Stop apologising all the time. This just makes us

feel weak. I'm not talking about when you bump into someone or if you have to interrupt two people talking because there is something that needs to be sorted out immediately. I mean when you allow yourself to get to the stage of saying 'sorry' all the time, to the extent that sometimes it seems that you are almost apologising for your very existence: 'Sorry that you didn't understand what I meant'; 'Sorry you didn't see my email yet'; 'Sorry for asking you a question'; 'Sorry that I am standing here in front of you' – and on it goes . . .

Seek assistance when you are too busy. If we always help out others, we need to be able to call in those favours when we are under pressure. Even if we are not all that busy, it can be good to practise asking for help. Before you start, though, it's good to be aware of what your brain will hit you with, perhaps something along the following lines: *I'll be a nuisance. They have their own work to do, they won't want to help me. It'll be an unfair burden on them. They'll think I'm weak and can't do my own job properly.* This is another situation where it can be really helpful to run through a Thought Record with yourself before beginning what you might initially find to be quite a challenging experiment.

Start taking ownership of your work. If you have done the bulk of the work on a project or presentation make sure that you are the person to front the demo. If we are always in the background, we will never get the exposure necessary to progress or to get the validation we deserve for all our hard work.

Stop playing down your importance to the team. This

one is linked to the previous point. It's about being fully cognisant of your skills and your role on the team. If in the beginning, you find it very difficult to talk yourself up, you can at least stop talking yourself down!

Know that it is not possible to be liked by everyone. Some people are just not going to be that into us. It doesn't mean anything about us – it just means that no one can be liked by all of the people all of the time. If we are in the habit of people-pleasing, we find it very difficult to tolerate someone not liking us. We react by putting all our efforts into a vain attempt to win over the unwinnable person, which can mean that we ignore everyone who is good to us and values us. It's better by far to let someone who doesn't like us go and focus on the people who do appreciate our input. If we hope to move into team-leading or management positions one day, it is crucial that we become more tolerant of people not being happy with us.

Stop believing that looking out for your own interests is selfish. If we do this 100 per cent of the time, then maybe it is, but it's unlikely that someone with a tendency to people-please will ever get to that stage. We need to bear in mind that we cannot hope to progress in the workplace if we are not self-interested to some degree.

Use the skills of the people-pleaser to progress. All that time spent focusing on others and considering their needs and interests first will have enabled us to develop some core people skills that can be very valuable, especially when leading a team. We tend to be very good at getting colleagues onside, bringing people together, building networks and enlisting people's help and cooperation, so that they actively want to work with us. These skills will be very valuable, when we decide to move forward with a little more self-interest. It's important to acknowledge that these are our strengths and incorporate them going forward.

A word of warning here: ironically enough, you will probably find that the people-pleaser in you will not go down without a fight. The one person your inner people-pleaser will stand up to is you! Prioritising your own needs can be very difficult, if it's something you're not used to. However, it is crucial to start and soon. Your career is not being served by constantly putting others first.

Dealing with difficult people

Something that caused me so much worry in my own working life, especially throughout my twenties when I worked in IT, was my inability to cope with a certain kind of person – the type whom I perceived as being an absolute tyrant.

In fact, early on in my career, I left a job because I just couldn't handle the constant fear I had going to work because I had to deal with a certain individual: the worry they caused me was relentless. This was the type of person who always just wanted the answers as quickly as possible and did not care about the circumstances – someone who always appeared to be angry, only gave praise sparingly and whose preferred method of engagement seemed to be conflict. When I started my next job, however, imagine my horror that there they were again. And the thing was, it turned out that they were in every organisation I ever worked in! They weren't always my manager or someone I had very close dealings with every time, but they were always there and they always caused me the same kind of difficulties.

I remember how during those times, I used to get so angry when the working day was over and when I was in the comfort and security of my own home, thinking about the injustice of it all. I would go over and over in my mind what I should have said, and what I would say next time. I spent hours thinking about all the terrible things I wished would befall the person and I spent so much time trying to figure out why they behaved the way they did. Why were they so cruel? Why were they not able to see how busy things were and how hard it was to have everything done all the time? Each time, however, as the next morning drew nearer, my anger ebbed away and was replaced by worry. Then when I got to work, I was terrified of any interactions I would have with them and I became a bumbling mess when I was in their presence. They were truly making my life a misery.

We need to remember that it's not what happens to us that matters, it's what we make it mean. This is a tough concept to get our heads around, because there can be so much that, we feel, *makes* us anxious, or angry or upset but, in reality, things just happen and we're the ones who add the meaning.

So, when it comes to a certain type of difficult person

at work, we might often think that they make our lives miserable, when in fact we can have a large part to play in both the making and the misery.

We can certainly decide that we have no responsibility for what is happening, that it is the disagreeable person who is the cause of our anxiety, and that their unpleasantness is something that has been inflicted on us and that we have to accept passively – but what then? If we take this approach, what power do we have to change the situation? We will just continue to live in a constant state of worry and make any and every future dealing with this person fraught with difficulty. What we need to do instead is look at our own role, acknowledge how some of the problem for us is psychological and a product of our own fears, and try to understand both that person and ourselves better.

Them and us

Let's say this disagreeable person is our boss. If we think about the situation as carefully and honestly as possible, is it accurate to say that their behaviour is always completely unacceptable? Or is it possible that our reaction to them might play more than a small part in the fraught relationship?

Before we delve into it any further, it's important to say here that, I am not talking about a person whose behaviour has crossed a line into bullying or singling someone out for harsh treatment or into any other non-negotiable territory. The kind of person I mean is one who is just focused on the job, unconcerned about others' feelings, and only interested in what they are looking for and whether we have it or not. They tend to just want to know the facts about the job in hand and have little patience for excuses or our reasons about why things are the way they are. They give no thought to whether they are being harsh and appear to have no problem with conflict, often seeing it as just a normal way of going about business. They seem indifferent to whether people like them or not. (OK, this may be somewhat of a caricature at this point, but it is roughly accurate in terms of the type of person who can have us in an absolute spin.)

It is not hard to see that if we are prone to worry, need to be liked and to get on with everyone, fear judgement and find conflict intolerable, then the difficult person will throw up all sorts of problems for us. If they are our boss or someone we have to work with closely, this is something we really need to address before worry takes over completely and every minute in the job is a living hell.

So, let's look at our role here and what better way we might go about interacting with a disagreeable boss or colleague.

The truth is that often we teach people how to treat us. If we go into a conversation in an anxious state, expecting to hear criticism and primed to react in a defensive way, then there will inevitably be an element of self-fulfilling prophecy in what ensues. The person in front of us can only view us as we have presented ourselves. If we have built up this person to be a monster, and worried so much in advance about the effect they have on us, then when we are around them, we are much more likely to get the response we dread and act in such a way that makes the situation worse. We may come across as meek and apologetic, stumble over our words and go blank when we are asked simple questions. This is not a way to build trust or portray confidence.

A new approach

Can we allow ourselves to regard every encounter with this type of difficult person as a neutral event, and trust that we will be able to deal with whatever comes up? This will enable us to be calmer in our approach, so we will have a clearer head to answer any question we are asked. We can also go into a conversation in a stronger, more assured manner.

This way of negotiating an encounter we may be dreading is really important, as it will give the other person a greater sense of confidence in us, since they will not misread our anxiety as incompetence or an inability to be direct and straightforward. If we fear that they do not see our value, then we will act from this place. The more we act from it, the more it prevents us from showing ourselves at our best and the more we believe we will never be able to satisfy the other person.

Looking at the hard evidence

To help us stop presuming that every interaction we have with the difficult person will be horrendous, how about we gather some concrete information and do some analysis – by taking the next, say, ten encounters with them as a starting point.

After each encounter, rate each one from one to ten, where one is totally fine and ten is absolutely terrifying. When you return to your desk after the encounter write down the rating and then tot up all the scores when you have reached ten encounters. In doing this task, you must enter the situation neutrally each time. You must not automatically assume a negative reaction from the person in question. What we are very likely to find is that the person we have built up to be a monster is actually completely fine most of the time, and that we have been allowing the one or two negative moments in our encounters with them to dictate how we judge them generally.

We also need to remember the role uncertainty has in our worry because even if we find ourselves giving some of the exchanges a low score, which make the person out to be not so bad, we will have seen them blow up on previous occasions, maybe even at us, and so there is a real possibility of this happening again in the future. It's like the one-armed bandit slot machines. We don't get the reward all the time, but every once in a while, we win. This reward, and especially the randomness of it, is what keeps people playing. This is a variation on the same concept that keeps us so afraid of difficult people, except that it's the penalty of their anger or unpleasantness that we will be at the receiving end of if we are unlucky enough – and that keeps our anxiety alive. However, we *have* to believe that we can handle that situation if it comes, and not live every encounter as if a bad outcome is inevitable.

In my own case, it got to the stage in my IT career where I knew I had to stop letting my fear of this kind of person have power over me. I realised as I have said earlier that such people are everywhere in the corporate world and also that the problem wasn't with them – it was with me. I reached this conclusion when I came up against yet another difficult person in a setup I was otherwise very happy with. When I decided I would just have to learn to live with this individual, I started to monitor my interactions with them, using the strategy outlined above.

What I found was that the vast majority of the encounters we had – ranging from short discussions and email interactions to longer meetings – were actually totally acceptable. Dotted here and there every so often were times when I felt they seemed agitated and were short with me, but I began to take those instances less personally, as I was beginning to see this as just the way this person was. As I became less fearful, I stopped seeing every upcoming interaction as one of inevitable conflict and I became more confident in my dealings with them. I was no longer sugar-coating bad news or apologising for my existence, and our interactions took on a new feel. There were still times when I perceived their responses as unnecessarily abrupt or irritated, but now, rather than getting caught up in the feeling of this being unfair, I just accepted it as part of their personality and not a reflection on me. For their part, the person in question seemed to also gain confidence in me and my abilities, and accordingly, the relationship between us became much easier.

Seeking validation

With difficult people in particular, we need to try to control our need for validation, especially when our instinct is usually to go into people-pleasing overdrive in our efforts to win these kinds of people over. If we are prone to seeking validation, we may value their praise above all else. We will do things that make us feel weak, just to get a smile, or some form of recognition or notice. We think we hate them, yet we laugh hysterically at their jokes. But the key point is that we must stop looking for their acceptance – not only because they cannot give us what we are looking for anyway but also because we have to stop giving them so much power.

If the feared person sends us an email looking for an answer, we need to learn to just send them a brief response with the answer. We do not need to send two detailed paragraphs as to why the answer is the answer – they do not want to read it. If they look for further clarification, we can send it of course. But we have to be aware of what we are doing in the long-windedness of our reply – which is trying to explain why the situation is the way it is in order to soften the blow of their perceived anger or make them see that we will bend over backwards in our efforts to help them. But, actually, the fact that they will have to sift through two paragraphs of excuses to try and find the answer is much more likely to bring on their anger! Nine times out of ten, they just want the information they asked for.

Paradoxically, the more we stop trying to impress such a person, the more respect they will have for us because we will also stop doing things that, in their eyes, make us look weak and possibly incompetent and inefficient. They have got to their position for a reason and maybe their personality type is an important part of the job they can do. This can be a useful lesson for those of us who are anxious when it comes to our turn to lead a team – not obsessing about what people think of us is actually quite a positive quality in a manager. It means they can lead, but also push back on pressure from above. At such time, it is helpful to not be overly empathetic and caught up in everyone else's story. A level of detachment can be helpful and a dogged focus on getting things over the line is often exactly what is needed.

Anxiety and work meetings

Work meetings are difficult for so many people. If the working environment is an amplifier of our anxiety, work meetings take it to the next level. Many elements of our fears can play out simultaneously. If we fear social situations, being found out, difficult people, not meeting our own high standards or reputational damage, here's a small room with no escape, and filled with people we may not know well or be comfortable with who are looking for answers we may not have. If we have an element of people-pleasing going on and our main concern is the other person being happy with us, this can be a very difficult space. If we like to avoid conflict at all costs, cannot abide not knowing an answer or not knowing if we will be able to hit deadlines, a meeting is often a place where some level of conflict is inevitable, and there is no way around it.

Over the past two chapters, we've looked at Impostor Syndrome, and how attention and concentration are greatly affected by anxiety. We've considered the role of worry and examined how perfectionism and the need to please others can add greatly to our fears and how dealing with a difficult person can cause us much pain. All of these elements can feed into our specific fears about meetings.

Social anxiety can feel greatly intensified when we are talking to a group of people. As in a non-professional social situation, we fear that a mistake or a misjudged comment may damage our reputations, make us look foolish or expose us for the fraud we believe ourselves to be – but all of this takes on even more significance in a professional setting.

When we start making a name for ourselves at a departmental level at work, we might become quite confident with our peers and those directly above us, but what happens when we move outside that bubble? There is something about having built a good reputation that can make meetings and presentations much more difficult. We have created expectations and now we have to live up to them. And what if we don't? Maybe our manager is in a meeting and they know how good we are and will rely on us to field questions, so they are likely to call on us to talk through things when needed. What if we make a mess of it? Maybe we've fooled our boss into thinking we're an expert in the field, but now we'll fall flat on our face and they will have to rethink everything they ever thought about us. There is an element of Impostor Syndrome at the root of this, mixed with a belief that we will inevitably mess things up and that that will be enough to change the opinions of those who know our worth.

Any work in tackling all the issues we've looked at in these chapters will greatly feed into our ability to deal more effectively with work meetings.

Below are some strategies you can use to help you navigate the very specific anxieties you may feel in relation to a particular upcoming meeting.

Changing our approach to meetings

We have seen previously how important it is to pin down exactly what we are thinking and feeling when we're anxious, rather than letting the anxiety continue to grow and intensify in a haze of uncertainty. If, for example, you are feeling anxious in the immediate run-up to a meeting because you are doubting your ability and ignoring the evidence of past meetings, where you acquitted yourself very well, then it can be useful to do a Thought Record (see page 98). If, however, your brain just keeps screaming danger, regardless of how much you reason with it, the thoughts probably need less attention and more defusion (see page 108). This is work you can engage in constantly to keep your thoughts at bay, and especially at times when your anxiety can be more intense.

For some, what we may be dealing with is anticipatory anxiety, where we are worried about the meeting and then, five minutes in, everything is fine. For others, the anxiety may persist throughout the meeting and often for some time afterwards. Either way, after we've addressed our thoughts in the crucial minutes directly before a meeting, it is our body that we need to be more aware of.

As we make our way to the meeting room, how are we feeling physically? If we are very anxious, we may have a sense of impending doom and our body reacts accordingly. Our threat system kicks in and we go into fight-or-flight mode. This is a time when it's very difficult to resist flight – and perhaps we might even pretend that we have to take a call or that we feel ill and have to leave – that's if we've made it as far as the room! However, how we chose to respond at moments like these is crucially important in terms of tackling anxiety.

When our minds scream at us to run, if we choose to listen and not go to the meeting, we have confirmed the danger to ourselves, and the next time we have a meeting it will be even more difficult to attend. We have to let our brains know that our physical reactions are not as relevant as it thinks. We can do that by paying attention to our bodies, and then going into, and surviving, the meeting.

Before you leave your desk and walk to the meeting, you need to anticipate your body's likely reaction to the event. Your breathing will become fast and shallow, your heart will start beating faster and you may become a little light-headed or nauseous. All of this is to be expected, and not treated as a sign that something is horribly wrong. So, you know what is coming and are ready to address it. Your breathing is probably the most important part. When you feel your breathing quicken as you approach the meeting room, begin the process of slowing it down. You are aiming to get to a place where you can count four seconds on the in-breath and four seconds on the out-breath. This might not be immediately possible, but you can build up to it, as you breathe in through your nose and out through your mouth. You can do this silently, and the people around you don't have to be aware of it.

Since, practically speaking, we cannot be breathing calmly if we are being chased by a predator, this process of slowing down your breath signals to the brain that the threat is diminishing. It can now lower the ancient threat system that is designed for acute physical emergencies and not Monday morning status meetings. You can then use some of the mindfulness techniques from Chapter 9 (Anxiety Toolbox III) to help with managing your thoughts. It is probably not a bad idea at this point to engage with someone besides yourself before the meeting starts, maybe just exchanging a greeting and a few words. This can take your focus off your anxious thoughts and body.

It's at key moments like these that all the work we have done so far comes into play. We've looked at and thought about Impostor Syndrome, perfectionism, people-pleasing, fear of difficult people, and so on. We're monitoring and addressing our thoughts. We know how our body reacts under stress and we know how to calm it. But, guess what? We may still feel anxious. We have to accept and let this be OK.

We have faced our anxiety and we are in the process of managing it. Now we have to be able to tolerate anxiety, in order to push through it. It is voluntarily facing our fears and allowing this to be a process that will pay dividends over time. It is in the brain's experiencing our surviving and coping with meetings that will allow the danger levels to be dropped.

When we can accept that managing and overcoming our fears is a process and not an instant off-switch, we can remove a lot of the suffering, annoyance and frustration that goes with constantly living with anxiety.

Chapter 9
Anxiety Toolbox III

By this stage, it is probably evident that when it comes to dealing with anxiety, managing our thoughts is a key part of the way forward, and that leaving them to sort themselves out is not an optimal long-term solution. It's about awareness coupled with the knowledge of what to do when we realise our habitual ways of thinking may not be working in our best interests.

Chapters 4 and 6 (Anxiety Toolbox I and II) outlined tools and strategies to help us tackle negative thought patterns, and we can use trial and error over a period of time to figure out which of them may be useful for us. Then, based on our actual experiences, we can begin to adapt and optimise these for our own needs and circumstances.

As we have success managing some thoughts, there

will be other challenges that throw us, and, of course, life is happening all the while too. Bearing in mind how progress with this kind of work really happens, with plateaus and spikes, we can remember that setbacks are all part of a bigger picture of moving forward.

This chapter will provide further tools and strategies for the management of our thoughts, including delaying worry, 'finishing out' (or following through) thoughts to their conclusion and learning to be more present. We will also look at how imagery can be used to help us see our thoughts as less threatening.

Delaying worry

Postponing and 'condensing' worry can be great ways of dealing with the intrusive nature of our thoughts.

Worrying gets in the way of problem-solving because it demands our full attention. Our minds cannot do two things at once and the anxious thoughts seem much more urgent to us because of the danger they are predicting. However, if we set aside a daily fifteen-minute period where we do nothing but indulge in our most worrisome thoughts, it can free us up during the rest of the day to get on with what we need and want to do with less noise and interference. So, maybe 8.00–8.15 p.m. every night is our worry time, and we treat this as one of the priorities of the day.

In preparation for your worry time make a note of all the things you want to worry about during the designated time. So, when an anxious thought or concern pops into your head at any time of the day, write it down. This is so that you don't forget any items on your 'worry list'; it also lets your brain know you are taking the worry seriously and that you'll be devoting time to it at 8.00 p.m. So, if you are going about your day and out of the blue get a worrisome thought that piques your anxiety, instead of getting caught up in that thought, the conversation in your head can go something like this: 'Ah, cheers, Brain, that's a beauty. I wouldn't have thought of it, had you not brought it up. I'll just jot it down so I don't forget it, and come eight o'clock tonight, I'll be all over it. For now, I've got to meet a friend for lunch, so let's go.'

This may sound ridiculous, but give it a go – it can be very powerful. It leaves you free to focus on the immediate issues at hand, safe in the knowledge that none of your worries will be neglected.

It also serves two other important purposes. Firstly, it creates a sense of separation between you and your thoughts. Where did the latest worrisome thought come from? You didn't summon it up or consciously decide to think about it. It just popped up out of nowhere. This is especially useful if the thoughts are personal, saying things about how weird or boring you are, or what people must think of you. This kind of thinking is much less powerful if you can see it as just random and not coming from some source of inner awareness that is inherently true.

The other benefit of postponing worry in this way is that it lets your brain know that you do not see the issue as being as relevant and dangerous as it does. Yes, it's something you are going to have a good worry about, but the very fact that you're putting it off till later in the day says a lot about its actual and immediate importance. Your brain gets to observe you acknowledging the worry and getting on with your day regardless.

So, when you get to 8.00 p.m., you can move to a designated spot, take out your notebook and start worrying about whatever is on the list. Some things will seem much less urgent than they did earlier on. And for the things that still pique your anxiety, you put the fifteen-minute timer on, buckle up and get to work. When the timer sounds – that's it, your worry time for the day is finished! You then move from the spot you picked to worry, and get on with your evening. This movement acts as a natural end to the task. Knowing your thoughts as you do now though, you expect that they are coming with you, but here you continue to practice not engaging: 'Tomorrow at 8pm we'll go again, but now we have people to meet'.

Playing the movie to the end

If we're used to worrying, we know we're never too far from some kind of fear about the future. Whatever is coming up, if there is any uncertainty at all, we'll always be sure to throw in a great big worst-case scenario. Fantastic. Not only that, though, we'll also continue fleshing out the thought, focusing on and further imagining the moment the worst possible outcome happens and we'll dwell on how utterly horrible it will be. However, we very rarely finish the thought by following it through to its final conclusion.

So, we might think about a project we have at work or a night out we have coming up, and we'll play out a fantasy where it all goes horribly wrong and we are the centre of the catastrophe. All eyes are on us: angry, unimpressed, judging. We then play that scene on loop for a good while until we are properly anxious. But why do we stop at the catastrophe? Why do we never play the script right to the end? There is surely much more that would happen afterwards, right? Might we be able to rectify the situation? Might there be some mitigating circumstances? Could we possibly handle the situation well or even, perhaps, learn something valuable to take forward with us?

It's like watching a horror movie and stopping it ten minutes from the end when the hero is at their most vulnerable and in mortal danger. If we keep watching, we'll find out that he escapes the situation and everything works out for the best. Instead, we leave the screen paused at the moment of impending doom and head to bed to mull over the awfulness of it all. So, instead of doing the equivalent with future fears – and stopping at the action at the moment of catastrophe – we need to keep going and expose ourselves to the full thought, by letting the entire scenario play out.

Why not try this as a thought experiment? Think of something that you are worrying about and that you have coming up soon.

Now, ask yourself the following questions:

> ⯈ What is the worst-case scenario in the worry
  you are thinking about?

» What would it mean if this actually happened?

» What would the next day look like?

» How would you cope?

» What do you have in your experience that would help you get through this?

» Do you know anyone else who has been here before?

» Do you have a support network you could lean on?

» Would this be a problem in five years' time?

» How likely is the worst-case scenario to happen?

» What is a more likely, or equally likely, scenario?

If we come to the conclusion that not only would the worst-case scenario be unlikely but that, even if it did happen, it would not be the end of the world and would be something we could cope with, is there any need to allow our entire evening or week or month to be hijacked by worry? This can be a good tool to use, together with postponing our worry.

Staying in the present

Mindfulness is a wonderful, scientifically proven way of bringing calm to our lives, whilst also enabling us to get more in touch with the present moment and learn to let our thoughts come and go in a non-judgemental way. It is not the same as being mindless – that would be following our thoughts without thinking – rather, it is noticing our thoughts and deciding how much attention we are going to give them. We learn to acknowledge thoughts and emotions as they arise, and let them be as and where they are – then, regardless of how strongly we experience them, we simply return to the present moment.

When most people think of mindfulness, they think of meditation – but mindfulness is all about being in the present moment, regardless of how we got there. Meditation is certainly a powerful way of doing this but, for those of us who might struggle to find the time or inclination, there are other approaches that can work well in calming the swirl of anxious thoughts.

When we worry, it is most often future-based – we get caught up in a fantasy world, leaving our current reality and thinking about things that will probably never happen. Our eyes are open, but we are not present. We are inwardly focused, missing everything that is going on around us. We have all experienced being with other people but feeling like we are miles away. There is no greater antidote to getting caught up in the future worry in our heads than being fully present in our immediate surroundings. This is where being mindful can be very powerful.

Whether you find yourself caught up in your thoughts or you feel anxiety in your body, you need to use this as your cue to return to the world around you. Worrying requires so much of your attention, so you need to find a way to anchor yourself to the present moment, where worry cannot exist.

One great way of doing this is to engage your senses.

If you are at your desk at work, look up. This will take you out of your inward focus. Stretch and look around, left and right. Turn and look behind you. What can you see? In your head, name all the things you can see. Are there any smells or can you taste anything? Stand up, if you need to. Really concentrate and try to name five different things you can hear (for example, traffic outside, other people talking, the clock, the air conditioning, your breathing).

Now, slowly rub your hands together and engage with the sound and sensation. Which is more prominent for you? Why is one more prominent than the other? Observe the lines on your hands. Are there more where the thumb meets the palm? Feel the texture of the skin on your hands. Are there any calluses? Are your hands softer or harder than you thought? Pick up a pen and run your fingers over its shape. You get the idea ... You are just looking to come into the present and anchor yourself there.

If you are in the car – for example, for the commute to work – this can be done whilst still being safe. In fact, it is probably safer to be as much in the present as possible, rather than driving absent-mindedly. Bring your focus to the things directly in front of you. What colours are the other cars you can see? What signs are you passing? Try slowly calling out everything you can see around you. Feel the texture of the steering wheel in your hand and become more aware of what you are doing with your feet, all the while keeping your eyes on the road. Take in the signs, take in the road, take in the distance between you and the car in front of you and the one behind you. Be aware of your surroundings in the most safety-conscious way. Become fully cognisant of everything around you, paying attention to other vehicles, bicycles, pedestrians, and so on.

When you have found the most effective way to hook yourself back into the present moment, you need to practise staying there. This can be the hard bit but it's important to know that, whilst staying in the present is the goal, it's the continual process of coming back to the present without judgement that you are training yourself in. The real power of mindfulness is in the continuing practice of coming back from your thoughts. The more you can learn to keep bringing yourself back to the real world, the better.

So, the practice of mindfulness goes something like this . . .

We find ourselves overtaken by worrisome thoughts and we acknowledge this to ourselves by naming these thoughts (e.g. 'worry thoughts'). We then begin to bring ourselves back into the present moment, perhaps using some of the approaches suggested above. We should not expect the anxious thoughts to stop demanding our attention or get upset when we find ourselves being inevitably sucked back into the story. We are not trying to *not* think these thoughts – that cannot be our goal. We are just training ourselves to come back to the present moment as soon as we become aware we have drifted off again.

So, you are driving to work and have strong anticipatory worry about the day ahead (the type that will probably lift after twenty minutes when you get there). When you become aware that you have been lost in your inner world for the past ten minutes - whether through the strength of your thoughts, feelings or bodily sensations - you acknowledge the thoughts and then use your senses to bring you back to the present. Five minutes later, you realise that you have been off in your head again, so you simply, and gently, bring yourself back to the present again.

Take a deep breath in and out. Feel the cool air entering through your nostrils and the warm air passing out through your lips. With an in and out breath counted as one, count these breaths up to seven. When you get to seven, start again. Notice how often you get lost in your thoughts and find yourself counting well past ten. Our thoughts will always demand our attention, but when we realise we have been caught up in them once more, we just reset to zero and start again.

It can be helpful here to draw on the analogy I used earlier - imagine your brain as a hapless puppy who keeps straying too far away. Each time you pick him up and place him at your feet again, rubbing his head and telling him to stay, you know full well that at first opportunity, he will be off chasing adventure again - and when he does, you will get up, walk over, pick him up and bring him back once more. Getting annoyed and hitting the puppy will not help the situation. Cursing your misfortune to ever get landed with a dog will not make him stay still. The more you patiently train him, the more he begins to 'get' it. As he gets older, he will be less likely to run off and, when he does, it will be easier to get him to return. That is why the repetition is worth the effort.

The brain is exactly the same. We have been indiscriminately following our thoughts wherever they take us for many years, so expecting not to have to constantly go after them now all of a sudden is futile. What you can do is begin the process of learning to be in the present. If for the moment, you can only achieve this fleetingly, then so be it. Staying in the present can be tricky. It is in the coming back from your thoughts that the real learning lies.

The wasp or the butterfly

Think about your worrisome thoughts. If you had to compare them to either a wasp or a butterfly, which would be a more accurate representation? The elegant, floaty, harmless creature or the angry, menacing pest? If one or the other was to land on your shoulder, how would you be most likely to react in each case? With the butterfly, chances are you might feel a sense of curiosity and interest. You might try to scoop it up and gently set it on its way, watching wistfully as it fluttered off and away from you. Afterwards, you might calmly return to what you were doing before it appeared.

On the other hand, if the wasp landed on you, it might elicit a stronger emotional reaction, as you flail about in a panicked attempt to get it off you. You might then watch it with contempt and suspicion until you are sure it is on its way and not coming back. You'd return to what you were doing previously, but be aware of a low-level simmering anxiety in your body. You could very well continue to occasionally scan the air for wasps for the rest of the afternoon, leaving you irritable and distracted. In truth, both creatures probably wanted very little to do with you, other than as a spot to rest for a moment's pause to observe their surroundings. One – the wasp – for sure poses a greater threat, but only if you start swinging at and agitating it.

As we gradually learn to separate ourselves from our worrisome thoughts, it would serve us much better to try and treat them as butterflies rather than wasps. When they inevitably arrive, swatting at them and then continuing to be on high alert in the aftermath is probably not ideal, if we are to change our relationship with our thoughts in the long term. Much like the wasp, they can appear to be filled with menace, but they will only cause us real pain if we anxiously engage with them. Can we treat them instead with the kind of curiosity we might have for the butterfly? Let them land where they like in the knowledge that they will likely float off again sometime soon and that if we allow them to do so, they will not cause us any real harm.

Chapter 10
Relationships and Anxiety – Part One

Romantic relationships can be tricky at the best of times. Whether we are in a relationship, out of one, have never been in one or are finished with them *forever*, they can occupy a lot of our headspace. Being single, navigating the dating scene, starting a relationship, meeting a new partner's friends and family, maintaining a relationship, going through a rough patch, breaking up, settling down, being in love, having doubts – wherever you are on the spectrum, there are complexities that can and will be made worse by unmanaged anxiety.

As we have seen previously, an overactive mind can be difficult enough when it's only our relationship with ourselves we have to contend with. When we are at any stage of a relationship with someone else, anxiety and worry and all that comes with them can add a layer of noise and confusion that clouds any situation, and can cause us to act in a way that does not make sense to ourselves let alone the other person. If we see the world through the eyes of anxiety, then small, seemingly insignificant events can take on much greater meaning. We can blow things out of proportion in a way that is difficult for the other person to understand, especially if we do not understand what is going on ourselves.

Awareness, as always, is key to understanding what is going on for us, and only from that platform are we able to decide on a course of action to bring about positive change. We have to become aware of what we are dealing with, and when we are acting from the skewed perspective of our anxiety, and not to the immediate situation in front of us. Very often, the situation is not the problem, it's what we make it mean that can cause unnecessary complications.

How we think is crucial in a relationship, because it will shape how we react in every situation. To know, therefore, why we are thinking the way we are is very important.

In this chapter, we will look at the typical relationship areas where anxiety can arise, the possible thought patterns and beliefs that drive the anxiety, and how to go about addressing the issues, so that we can manage our emotions in a way that will benefit both ourselves and the relationship.

The honeymoon period

The beginning of a relationship – the first three or four weeks – can be a magical time. There is nothing more exciting than getting to know someone who we find attractive and interesting, and who shows a similar interest in us. Both parties are putting their best selves forward, and time with the other person is at the top of both of their priority lists. For a brief moment, anxiety quietens as our focus is redirected. But don't worry, normal service will resume shortly!

The 'don't-mess-this-one-up' worry

For the worriers, this early stage of a relationship can be a blessing and a curse. There is the new and exciting, which gives our thoughts something else to focus on, but with that comes the monster of uncertainty. *What if they are not as into me as I am into them? Do I hold back or jump in? I don't want to get hurt. What if I'm not as into them as they are into me? How would I get out without hurting them? What if I don't like their family or friends? What if they don't like mine? How will I know if this is love or not?*

On top of our general, future-based worries relating to ourselves and how we will handle things, there is also the interaction with a person we are just getting to know, and this can throw up its own difficulties. Misinterpreting a person's actions, what they say or don't say, how they interact with other people, reading things into their likes and dislikes – these can all play a part in the 'what if' thoughts in our head. Sometimes, if our own self-image isn't that healthy, we can even question the soundness of mind of a person who seems to like us!

Hopefully by this stage of this book, you have begun to do some work around uncertainty. If not, Chapter 3 (Worry) may be a good place to start.

Uncertainty and the need for control drive worry. When dealing with another human being, especially in the early stages of a relationship, certainty will be thin on the ground. If we let our need to know how they feel about us or our need for control to take over, we can drive the other person away. If we choose a person who is compliant and gives us a level of certainty, those traits may drive us mad in the not-too-distant future because our need to be challenged will not be met.

One great thing we can do to help us manage early-stage relationship worries is shrink the timeframe right down. In Chapter 4 (Anxiety Toolbox I), we looked at playing with our timeline either to gain perspective or keep our focus on the here and now. In this instance, it might help us to stop running off too far into the future. How is the relationship today? Does it feel good? *All I know is that things seem to be going well at the moment.* Can you ignore your brain's cautionary tale about the future – e.g. *I cannot tell what will happen down the road or how this will work out, and I don't trust that I won't scare the living daylights out of myself with thoughts of disaster and inevitable hurt.* The less you engage with negative speculation about the future, the better.

When it comes to future-based everything-is-going-to-end-badly thinking, we need to defuse from those thoughts and let our minds know we are not going to react, whilst also staying as present in the current moment as we possibly can. *I'm enjoying this relationship at the moment, Brain. You can hang with us and keep shooting me the disaster thoughts if you like, but we're going to the cinema, so keep it down.*

As we saw before, the moment we let our brain know we concur with its 'danger' thoughts, the more of these thoughts it will throw our way in an effort to protect us. The less we engage with the thoughts, the more our brain will treat the situation as not being of immediate urgency, with the result that, over time, such thoughts will become weaker and more muted.

It may also be a good time to hand these worries over to your future self (see page 115). As such, you become more comfortable with the idea that Future You will be able to deal with any situation that actually arises. When your brain tries to hit you with the usual 'what if' thinking, you can come back with something like: *Yeah, Brain, I'm not sure either, but I'm sure Future Me will be able to deal with it.*

Using these strategies should make it easier for us to just be in the relationship in the present, and let that be enough, enjoying our time with the other person during this precious period, whilst trying as best we can to manage the worry. We acknowledge that we don't know how the relationship will pan out, but we can allow ourselves to turn down the volume on the constant speculation and know that whatever happens in the future, we will be able to cope with it.

Find love, give it everything you've got, break up – rinse and repeat

The honeymoon period can be so magical and there can be a real sense of excitement and expectation in the early days. For some of us, when the inevitable slowdown comes and the first choppy waters need to be navigated, we can feel let down, anxious or disappointed with the way things are turning out. If we always need the buzz of the new and we cannot tolerate this natural transition into a more realistic phase of the relationship, we may see this as an irreparable fault in the dynamic between both parties and decide to end things prematurely. Perhaps this is the way all our relationships have gone – when things begin to get difficult, they end, leaving us generally disillusioned with love, feeling that it just isn't for us and that we will never be able to connect properly with another person.

The reality is that in the honeymoon period of any relationship, we are not going out with the person in front of us, we are going out with a fantasy. We project onto them everything we want in a romantic partner because we don't really know them yet – and they are doing the same with us. Both parties are showcasing their best qualities and holding back the parts of themselves they think might be less than desirable. Slowly, as we get to know the other person better, and they show more of their true selves, the real person and our fantasy will often be at odds.

If we are not prepared to let go of the fantasy and deal

with the sometimes tricky challenges of relationship building, then this will be a difficult space to navigate. Perhaps we begin to catastrophise about small things that have been newly revealed, and rush to conclude that we cannot see a future with this person or perhaps we are angry with them for destroying our fantasy and we may feel they have somehow let us down.

A very modern dating anxiety – too many choices

Working through this type of thinking at the early stages of a relationship can be tough - and seems to have been made tougher still by the advent of modern dating technology. While it is amazing that we can now meet people so easily, and that these days, so many of us find love through online technology, it does seem to have its drawbacks too. If, for example, we tend to have difficulty when the honeymoon period is over, then the ready access modern dating sites give us to an apparently unlimited number of potential partners can have a particularly negative effect.

How do we even pick a partner when there seem to be unending possibilities and options? In his book, *The Paradox of Choice: Why More is Less*, eminent US psychologist and academic Barry Schwartz argues that having too much choice can cause paralysis, and that the more choice we have, the unhappier we will be after a decision.

Our final choice will necessarily come under much more scrutiny than if our options had been limited. The expectations we place on the partner we do decide upon are also much higher, as this person has to go up against the fantasy of all the people we let go. Schwartz suggests that the fact we had so many partners to choose from may take away from the actual happiness we feel with the one we chose, as we will think about what we might possibly have missed out on, which can even lead us to blaming ourselves for the final decision.

With such easy access to one another and with the old barriers of having to approach someone or wait to be approached removed, internet-dating options have thrown up problems that we humans may not have had to struggle with before. Certainly not to the extent we do today, anyway. We may now routinely find ourselves in the early stages of a relationship with more than one person. So how do we work that out? And what if we get it wrong? If things do not pan out exactly as we want, we can end the relationship and just dip back in to the sea of unlimited possibilities. Some of us might find it difficult to commit to one person, when we can be constantly experiencing the new and exciting, the buzz of the chase, the possibility of finding the perfect partner. And how do we deal with the fact that the person we are with also has unlimited possibilities from which to choose? How do we compete?

Yet our fantasy of the perfect person is most likely just that – a fantasy. Someone who meets our every need and is caring and exciting, who wants to be with us and yet knows when to give us space, someone we always get on with, have great fun and even better sex with, who shares our interests, outlook and values . . . If we cannot accept the reality that we will never find someone who ticks all the boxes, but continue to look for the impossible, then we are putting ourselves in a tricky position.

Beyond the honeymoon period

When the clouds appear in the honeymoon period, this can actually be the opportunity for real intimacy to begin. By this time, we are seeing a truer version of the other person and they are seeing a more realistic version of us. We may have learned a lot about our partner before this – but how accurate was it really? Perhaps they were putting their own needs and wants to the background or overlooking a lot of our nonsense, purely because they too were caught up in the magic of the early stages.

When building a relationship, a good starting point is to presume we have no idea what the other person wants or what they need to feel loved. This place of ignorance enables us to go about finding out who they really are, without any preconceptions. It is this accepting of the other, warts and all, that can lead to real closeness. We can then begin a negotiation process, where we put forward what we want and expect from a partner and we hear out our partner on their terms too. It's most likely not just one conversation, but an ongoing discussion over a long period of time, as sometimes what we think we want is not what we want at all. It's in the negotiation, the listening, the compromise and the evolving of the relationship that we will figure that out.

When the honeymoon period ebbs away and if we remain committed to the furthering of the relationship, it is helpful to be aware of the role anxiety can play in our reactions and decision-making, and the different psychological problems we may subsequently face. There are so many areas that can trigger worry, but, with a little awareness on our part, these need not be the big deal we sometimes make them out to be. If, with time, we can work on both becoming aware of our triggers and softening our responses to them, whilst, on the far side, being able to tackle the 'what ifs' when they hit us, then we will be much better placed to relax into building a strong relationship, with less noise and drama from our thoughts.

As we seek to build solid bonds, what can be helpful is to see the other person as a human being who is as complicated as we are. They have their own stuff going on. They often react impulsively without knowing why. They will have values, beliefs and rules that they may not be aware of, but which will be driving their decisions and actions. Jumping to conclusions, or presuming we understand the thinking or motives behind a person's actions can be a major cause of unnecessary worry or hurt. We have been so long with our own ways of thinking that we sometimes presume the rest of the world thinks exactly as we do. We need to stop seeing our partner's actions and decisions through the lens with which we view the world ourselves.

If we acknowledge our differences and allow for the other person to be coming from a different angle, then it can give us perspective. For example, if we come from a family where swearing was seen as very disrespectful, and our partner comes from a background where this was just part of normal conversation, this might be a source of conflict, if we judge the way the other person talks to us as disrespectful. If we were to tell someone to **** off, it would mean something pretty drastic but, for our partner, maybe it is just a throwaway comment.

Likewise, if we come from a family where humour, slagging, mocking and constantly ribbing each other was the norm, it may cause a lot of friction if we are with someone who doesn't operate in this way. They may enjoy some of the fun and lightening of the mood that this approach can bring, but at a certain point get tired of the constant jokes at inappropriate times, if this is how we learned to deal with difficult conversations. We might be left thinking that our partner can't take a joke, while they feel exasperated that we just can't be serious sometimes.

If we can open up a dialogue where we are both willing to look below the surface and share what we find, it can really help ease conflict both in the moment and going forward. The ability to see things from the other person's point of view is clearly a very valuable skill when building a relationship. Talking and paying attention are key components to this skill.

As we move past the honeymoon stage, we have to quieten our thoughts, shrink the timeline and stop catastrophising. Doing this will enable us to manage anxious thoughts as we allow ourselves to get past the exciting early days of being with our partner, and learn to build tolerance for the things we may have historically run away from.

In Chapter 11, we will look at the key areas where worry and anxiety can make it more difficult to negotiate in a long-term, committed relationship, as well as how we can best approach and begin to improve these.

External anxiety and how it affects a relationship

In this chapter, we have seen how an anxious mindset can play out in the way we relate to a significant other, especially in terms of the kinds of fear that can make the beginning of a relationship difficult to navigate.

We need to also consider how being generally anxious about many other areas of our lives can impact on both people in a key relationship. Anxiety can, as we know, be all-consuming, and if, for example, we have a tendency to worry a lot about work, we have to be mindful that this may unwittingly spill over into our relationship and cause difficulties for our partner as well as ourselves. Anxiety can keep us locked in our own heads or seeking constant escape from the suffering that goes with it. This can leave us so caught up in our own inner struggles that we may be blind to the way those who love us are affected.

When someone is in the grip of anxiety, they will often become detached and difficult to reach. There may be many reasons for which we do not want to talk about what is going on for us. Perhaps we see being vulnerable and opening up as a sign of weakness or we feel that our struggle with anxiety should be something we can handle on our own. Perhaps we feel that if we let down our guard and let things out, we would simply fall apart and never be able to get ourselves back together again. Maybe we don't want to burden our partner with our problems or we fear that their opinion of us will change if they know what is really going on in our inner lives. Maybe to talk about things would mean having to confront the fear, which is often the last thing we want to do. Whatever the reason, it can be difficult for our partner to see us struggle and not feel able to help.

Even if we are open to talking and being with the other person, we can appear distant. We may have decided that, since we have been with our anxiety all day, we will give ourselves a break from the constant thoughts when we are with our partner. Unfortunately, our minds may not be on the same page with this plan, and so, while we do our best to engage in conversation about other things, we are clearly not fully present as our anxious inner monologue continues to plague us. This kind of anxiety can cause our nerves to be frayed and our patience short, leaving us sensitive and fragile, or touchy and snappy. At times like these, it can be difficult for our partner to understand that things which would normally be insignificant are making us unusually upset or disproportionately angry.

It is important for us to be aware of what the knock-on effects of our anxiety might be for the other person. Regardless of how patient and supportive they are, we can still try to be mindful of how our issues are playing out in the relationship. Are we reacting to what is going on in front of us or are we reacting to the anxiety that has taken over our thoughts? When we begin to tackle anxiety and figure out the source of what is happening for us, we will be able to tell the difference more easily.

Say, for example, we are feeling very anxious, but we are still in the hazy stage of not understanding exactly why. We are on edge and seeking comfort rather than challenge. Our partner might pick up that something is off but may not want to broach the subject. They then say something absentmindedly, which feels to us like exactly the wrong thing to say, and now we are either narky with them or withdraw into ourselves.

This awareness can be difficult if we are in the early stages of learning to manage anxiety and may be a hindsight operation for a period of time. We react out of our heightened emotions at the time, and only later can we figure out what happened. In this process, we'll need our self-compassion and curiosity to kick in: 'OK, I reacted pretty strongly there – what just happened?'

As we continue to work this through on a number of occasions, we can begin to be more aware of our thoughts and emotions before we act blindly from them. If we sense that we are already feeling anxious, we can let our partner know we are dealing with something and that we may need a bit of patience. We can also try to give our partner the benefit of the doubt in situations where we are unsure why they have said or done something that upsets us.

This is why it is so important to tackle our anxiety.

As we have seen throughout this book, it can spill into every aspect of our life, including our most important relationships, and if we are reacting to our partner with emotions that do not seem to fit the situation, then they will be likely to begin to react to our reaction. And before we know it, the relationship is a source of anxiety that it wasn't before - which is of course the last thing we need when we are already struggling!

Low mood

It is not uncommon for low mood to be a direct result of unmanaged anxiety. After a period of sustained worry and stress, everything becomes too much all at once, and we start to withdraw into ourselves as we struggle with trying to figure out why we are feeling down. As discussed in the early chapters of this book, it may feel as if the mood has hit us suddenly, but it may well have been building over a long time. So, while we increase our agitation by trying to pinpoint an event that triggered everything, it was in fact most likely a culmination of several things. This is why it is crucial that we can come out of the fog of our thoughts and start to tackle our difficulties head-on. If we can do this, things will become easier and life will seem brighter for both ourselves and those we love.

With this in mind, for the good of our relationships as well as for our own health, we have to be watchful for when our coping reservoir (see Chapter 2) is becoming full and we are going through a period where our anxiety is on high alert and small things are more difficult to handle. This, as we know, is a time when we can very quickly become overwhelmed, which can in turn leave us feeling lethargic and low. We may not notice that we are withdrawing from our partner, as we show less enthusiasm for everyday events, but they have to live with our mood and are likely to feel there is nothing they can do to help, especially when we do not know what is going on ourselves. If left unaddressed, this build-up of anxiety and the resulting low can definitely take its toll on our relationship.

There, but not there

Anxiety and escape can go hand in hand (and this is something we'll look at in depth in Chapter 13). If our partner can be that escape from our anxiety, so that when we are with them we are able to get a break from our anxious thoughts and feelings, then great – but, so often, we don't let in those closest to us, because we feel we don't want to burden them or we fear they might think less of us. If we use other forms of escape, however, and this is interfering with our relationship, then it may be worth checking how much time we spend with our partner whilst fully engaged. It is also worth keeping an eye on how this affects all our relationships, as family and friends will be experiencing our distancing also.

When we are trying to escape unwanted feelings, because we are too afraid to face them head-on, the methods we use have to be powerful enough to remove us completely from present reality. They need to enable us to break out of our heads and numb us to the fears and the feelings we are running from. So, the likelihood that we can be present for our partner at these times is very slim indeed. And the greater our need for escape, the more time we will be spending on these activities and away from loved ones – whether physically or emotionally or both.

One absolute powerhouse as a means of escape is social media. Always available, reliably there, always soliciting our attention if we are away from it for too long, it is the perfect short-term fix for an anxious mind. Unsurprisingly, those of us suffering from anxiety can easily fall into a routine of getting lost in social media. Often, it is the first thing we turn to in the morning and it is a constant presence throughout our day. If we are using it to escape from anxious thoughts, we will begin to turn to it more and more, as we continue to ignore our fears and leave unwanted feelings unaddressed.

When used in this way, social media will not only rob us of our time: being constantly online will also put a wall between us and our partner, where we may be present, but are not available to them. This can give a clear message that we do not care enough about someone to stick around and engage and that we would rather be reading about everyone else's lives or getting caught up in the latest trending subject. When we are constantly allowing ourselves to be pulled away from an opportunity for communication and intimacy with the person we are supposedly closest to, it can quickly feel like there is a third party in the relationship. Here we could of course replace social media with anything from alcohol and drugs to video games, pornography, TV – or any of the other things we do to excess at the expense of real contact and intimacy. It is not about the means of escape we choose, but the fact that we insist on escape.

A huge aspect of managing anxiety is about being able to disengage from short-term behaviours that give us momentary relief, but which cause us more difficulties in the long run. We need to start choosing behaviours that may be less comforting but actually present us with long-term solutions. Being able to communicate and navigate tough negotiations is integral to building a strong relationship – but, above all, we need to be present.

Expectations of our partner

If anxiety is an ongoing part of our lives, we need to think about what expectations we have of our partner in this regard. It's an important thing to consider, especially if we have decided to tackle our fears. We may be very open about what is going on for us or we may be more guarded – but, either way, our partner will have a part to play in how we take things forward. That's what relationships are about. All our quirks and oddities will come up against all the quirks and oddities of the other person and, as a couple, we have to figure out together a way to co-exist.

However it manifests for us, anxiety can be difficult to understand, for someone who has never experienced it. As well as this, not everybody has the same level of empathy. If we are the kind of person who feels everyone else's pain and can empathise easily, we need to realise that not everybody has that capability. If your partner does not understand what you are going through, allow them to not understand. All we can do is ask for love and support when we are struggling.

If it is worries or intrusive thoughts that are causing us to suffer and disengage, it can be difficult for another person to truly appreciate the power they can have and how, even when at their most illogical, to the sufferer these thoughts feel very real. If it's social anxiety we struggle with, our partner may have got to know and love a person who they cannot believe has difficulties in social situations. As they do not have access to all our thoughts, they may not see the person we feel we are.

We cannot get hung up on a partner 'not understanding' or sometimes getting annoyed or impatient with us for our worries. Can we see it from their point of view? If they are supportive and try to understand, wonderful – but we need to recognise that this isn't possible for everyone and, more importantly still, that this is our fight. We can let a partner know what we are going through or that we are trying to change things and communicate what we need from them – but the more we rely on another person to bolster us up or do the work for us, the longer it will take to overcome our fears.

The bottom line in all of this is that, no matter what stage we are at in a relationship, an ongoing problem with anxiety will undoubtedly play a role in how we relate to the other person. If we can become more aware of when we are acting from anxiety, and how this impacts on our partner and the relationship in general, we will be more able to make better choices and have a different conversation than if we have no idea why we are acting as we are. Our partner is perfectly placed to be both a support and an escape from our worries, but we have to be able to let them in and know when our anxiety is keeping them out.

Chapter 11
Relationships and Anxiety – Part Two

Relationships and oversensitivity

It is not uncommon for those who struggle with anxiety and worry to also be empathetic and sensitive in their dealings with others. Being sensitive can be a wonderful thing, as we can be very much in tune with the emotions of others and sufficiently in touch with our own feelings to be able to offer real listening and support to those we are close to. Others may turn to us when they are struggling and our partner can find our willingness and ability to be there for them a source of real comfort.

It's when we are oversensitive that difficulties can arise in relationships. A partner can often find themselves walking on eggshells around us, choosing their words carefully or holding off altogether from saying things that bother them for fear that it will lead to an overreaction or a closing down of communication. It can be exasperating to live this way, especially if a lovely day or time spent together is ruined in the blink of an eye because of what might seem like an overreaction to the smallest of things.

From our side of the fence, it can be a painful experience to feel criticised constantly, let down or judged. If we are oversensitive, we may feel we are continually at the mercy of our emotions and the whims of the other person, who can hurt us with a throwaway comment, a sigh or an uninterested look. We may read meaning into actions where no such meaning exists and interpret any remark as criticism, regardless of our knowledge of the actual intention. This way of being can play on our nerves and further ramp up our anxieties about the relationship and the future.

So, there are two difficult questions that it's important to look at. Firstly, how do you know if it is you who is oversensitive or if your partner is being too harsh or critical? Secondly, if you conclude that you are the one being too sensitive, what can you do about it?

Is it them or me?

This can be a tough one. We might be fully aware that we tend to overreact to things or, equally, we may not recognise this in ourselves at all. If we are oversensitive and it is not something we are aware of, it may be a way of reacting we have had all our lives and so we do not see it as a problem or understand how we could be any different.

Perhaps we had overcritical parents and this way of being is a natural response to our upbringing. If we grew up in an environment where criticism was ever-present, we may have become accustomed to hearing criticism in everything. Or perhaps it was an environment where putdowns were dressed up as humour and nothing was said directly, but only ever implied, so, as adults, we find we are often stung by jokes that were not intended to hurt. Maybe when we were growing up, we experienced being let down continually and so any hint of someone not coming through for us now leaves us upset and wanting to withdraw. In one sense, it doesn't really matter what the cause is or was, what matters now is that if we are constantly looking for ways to be hurt, we may find them in the most innocuous of situations.

There are certainly people out there who are overly critical, constantly putting others down and being quite manipulative in how they try to control the narrative around who is misinterpreting what. Maybe we are even attracted to people who are critical or who are harsh in their reactions because, at an unconscious level, this may feel somehow more familiar and comfortable to us because of our experiences early in life.

When we are attempting to manage anxiety and change the way we engage with our fears, it is important to be able to step back and think about things a little more objectively. We can start by asking ourselves some key questions. *Do I tend to hear criticism a lot in the relationship or does my partner think I am oversensitive? Do I trust them to be truthful with this assertion? Is there a recurring theme here – have I heard the same things from other partners or friends before?* If we feel we react badly to what others say or do more than other people we know or we are regularly upset by what people say, there may be a case to be made for our being oversensitive.

It might be a good idea to reach out to a trusted friend at this time if necessary. Can they shed any light on this for us? Do they see us as oversensitive? Do we tend to take a lot of things personally? We may have to let them in on what we are trying to figure out and assure them that we will not take their answer personally because if we actually are oversensitive, our friends may not be keen to tell us uncomfortable truths!

So, after this analysis, you might discover that, yes indeed, you can be oversensitive at times. If it is very difficult to know whether it is you or your partner, maybe you can work on oversensitivity anyway. If you are constantly reacting to your partner in a way that makes you anxious or upset, it might be worth a go. In any case, it will certainly not be a waste of time to make yourself more robust in the face of the actions and comments of other people.

What now?

Like everything that involves change at a non-surface level, the next steps will be a process. There may be much learning from experience involved. We will not just stop being too sensitive overnight, as we have no doubt been this way for a long time. It will be about making small adjustments, seeing how they work, allowing it to be uncomfortable, pushing through, making more changes, facing fears, stepping back and going over the same ground again.

Compassion, curiosity and patience will be important components as you try to unpick what is really going on for you. If you can bring your partner on board with the plan, then that would be wonderful, but it is not vital. If they know that you are going to be trying to deal with oversensitivity and that you need some understanding and patience in this time, it would be helpful – but you can also do this work without their participation or awareness of what you are doing.

Over the next while, observe your interactions with your partner and keep track of the occasions when you reacted in a manner that could be deemed oversensitive. When you identify the triggers, you can do an exercise on why you reacted so strongly to them:

Take out a pen and paper – or you can also just do this exercise mentally. Say, for example, it is perceived criticism that sets you off. Where do your thoughts go when you think of being criticised or put down? What thoughts or images come to mind? We can often feel as if we are being told off and are left feeling childlike. We may also identify feelings of anger or humiliation in ourselves. Do you feel shame when you are wrong or make a mistake? Why are you so averse to criticism and so ready to react? Do you associate it with unfairness or injustice?

How about the feeling of being let down by someone – what does being let down mean to you? Does it bring up strong emotions? Does it mean anything about the relationship with that person or the future? Maybe it feeds into an assumption you have that others will always let you down. If we are looking out for this, we are likely to find it where it may not have been intended. Does it say anything to you about yourself? Do you believe you are worth being there for?

If we are driven by a need to be needed, then any sign to the contrary will fill us with a fear that we are no longer valued. If we struggle with our own self-worth, every sigh or unimpressed look stokes a fear that others see us as unimportant. If we have a fear of being left alone, then every small perceived rejection will be amplified. How about a fear of being controlled or of being dependent, a fear of being seen as useless? Whatever we find, it's important to know that we may be acting from this place and not taking the situation in front of us at face value.

When we identify the kinds of situation we tend to take too personally, we can then take note of what form our reaction takes. Do we go into ourselves and sulk or do we explode and shout and argue? Or maybe we react in a different way. Maybe it's immediately obvious to us or maybe we have to look out for it over the days afterwards, really paying attention to how we are feeling and acting.

When we know what we are looking for and we know how we react, we can go about the task of challenging some of the thinking that is driving the oversensitivity. In the early stages of this process, we will be doing most of the cognitive work after the event, as it will probably be too difficult, initially anyway, to do this work in the midst of a strong emotional response to something that was said or done.

Here we are going to need a Thought Record (see page 98) and take a look at a situation after it has occurred. There can be any number of situations that kick off our reaction; below are a few examples of potential triggers:

» Our partner is doing something (e.g. cooking or putting together some flat-pack furniture) and they snap at us impatiently for getting in the way when we try to help.

» While we are telling them how to do something, our partner seems uninterested or distracted.

» Our partner points out something about us that bothers them.

» We spend a couple of hours cleaning the apartment. When our partner comes in, they jokingly point out something we missed.

» When we ask them to do something for us or to help us with something, they sigh audibly.

» Our partner makes a joke about something we are wearing.

» We show affection to our partner and they seem to ignore it.

↠   We have plans to meet up with our partner but
     they cancel because their friends have just got
     into town.

You might look at the above list and think, *Yes, the partner
in question is being kind of annoying in all those instances.*
The important issue though is that when something like
this happens for us are we able to point out that we're a
bit irritated and move on – or does the incident become
something much bigger than it needs to be?

If we are too sensitive, we'll likely have one of two
responses. Either we'll withdraw into ourselves and sulk
for a period of time, ruminating on the horrible thing that
was said or done and not knowing how to get out of our
mood, forcing our partner to come to us and make things
OK. Or we'll explode and shout at our partner, leaving them
in a place where they have to react and ask themselves
how we got to here from such an innocuous event.

After an event that we decide we have reacted too
strongly to, a good time to sit down and run the situation
in question through a Thought Record is whilst the
feelings are still strong. Let's take the example from
the trigger list, where we have spent time cleaning
the apartment, and our partner jokingly points out
something we missed.

THOUGHT RECORD

THE SITUATION

Partner jokingly pointed out something I missed after
my clean-up.

MY EMOTIONS

Hurt: 70%, Upset: 60%, Annoyed: 50%, Frustrated: 50%

MY THOUGHTS

I can't believe they had the nerve to point that out, after I gave up the afternoon to clean the place.

I do so much for them and they don't even notice.

They never appreciate anything I do. They always criticise me.

I give so much in this relationship and don't get half as much back.

I never criticise anything they do.

I always try to be so supportive, I wish they could give me the same support back.

I shouldn't have bothered – they don't even care.

I wish they could see how hurtful they are being.

EVIDENCE FOR MY THOUGHTS

They quite often don't notice everything I do around the apartment.

They can say things quite absentmindedly at times.

They can often say hurtful things.

I am always putting them first and doing my best.

EVIDENCE AGAINST MY THOUGHTS

I realise I do a lot to please them that they might not even know I do.

I never tell them about all I have done, I just expect them to notice and praise me.

Maybe I do more than they do, but it could be just a habit we have fallen into.

It's true I never criticise them, but I do need to talk more because if I don't, I can end up being punishing in other ways - whether that be through silence or smart remarks.

They do care, it just doesn't seem like it in the moment.

They probably don't know it hurts so much because I never tell them.

BALANCED THOUGHTS

What they said was annoying, but they probably didn't know I was working all afternoon - and maybe they were just trying to help. If it bothers me so much and it happens again, I might have to say something rather than bottle it up. Maybe we need to have a talk about the splitting up of the chores, as I seem to do much more and this needs to change.

MY EMOTIONS

Hurt: 50%, Upset: 50%, Annoyed: 30%, Frustrated: 20%

As we pointed out before, we will not get rid of the feelings entirely, but we can try to reduce them to a more manageable state.

We will probably have to go through the process a number of times - i.e. do a Thought Record to try and get a handle on our thoughts and finding some balance and perspective. When we have more experience, we can begin to integrate this way of looking at things into our way of thinking. The idea is that we catch our overreactions earlier and earlier each time, forcing ourselves more quickly out of our post-event rumination and into a more appropriate response. If we feel we need to apologise afterwards to the other person for our reaction, then so be it. If a conversation is needed about the other person's behaviour, then that is something we can also do. With enough practice and experience, it will get to the stage where we can snap ourselves out of the reaction quite quickly after the event.

Allow this to be a slow process, as it is difficult. We can bring in some defusion (see page 108) from the thoughts, with some compassion and curiosity: 'Ah, here's the I've-been-let-down-story again. Wow, it's mad how strong this feeling is for me, it totally took control there for a few minutes.' After we manage to separate ourselves from the thoughts, we can then step out of our heads again, and resume the interaction with our partner.

People-pleasing in a relationship

In Chapter 8 (Anxiety in the Workplace – Part Two), we examined the role people-pleasing has in fuelling anxiety in the workplace. Within a relationship, this tendency can manifest itself in similar ways, but it can have even deeper ramifications when the focus of our attention is just one person.

Many of my clients have been struggling with an overriding need to put others before themselves. They continually give of themselves, expecting nothing in return. Choices they make will always be with the other in mind. They may sacrifice time with friends and family to always be there for their partner, even when it is not something their partner requires or expects.

There can be huge guilt associated with putting ourselves first.

Let's think about that for a minute . . .

Guilt usually comes about when we know we have done something wrong. For some people, choosing their own needs over those of others can bring up such negative feelings that they feel as if it is morally wrong. Related to this is the belief that putting others first is the right thing to do and that this makes us a 'good' person. We can also have a fear that if we do not give people what we think they want, they could become angry or reject us – so we give up our own needs to appease the other person. This can quickly turn into letting the other person control us, as we will do anything to stave off anger or rejection.

Whilst it is true that an amount of selflessness, especially in a relationship, can be a good thing, there is certainly a balance to be struck. Unfortunately, when it comes to people-pleasers, balance in this area can be in short supply. If we are too agreeable and over-empathise with other people's emotions, we are likely to want to protect and take care of our loved ones, regardless of whether they need protecting or not. We may feel unable to tolerate the pain of others or the guilt that comes when we are not tending to their needs.

There are many ways this tendency to people-please can play out with a partner. In the early stages of a relationship, for example, we may be much more concerned with what the other person thinks of us, rather than whether they are a suitable partner. We throw ourselves headlong into the relationship, eager to win affection and gain approval – often ignoring signs that they may not be right for us. The other person may be bowled over by our attention and commitment, as we feed off the glow of their acceptance and burgeoning love. Of course, it is not uncommon at the beginning of any relationship to want to put the other person first, but this is the default position for the people-pleaser, even after the initial stages.

The end of the honeymoon period can be particularly difficult for the people-pleaser, as conflict, in some shape or form, inevitably begins to materialise. In the ongoing negotiation that follows, if we are more concerned about the needs of the other person, then any vision of a joint future will be heavily skewed in one direction. This may seem fine, and even preferable, if the other person's needs are our sole focus, but it is not a solid foundation for a long-term relationship where both partners are supported, engaged, challenged, fulfilled and equal.

Whether we feel our needs are important or not, we still have needs, and if they are never being fulfilled, we can end up feeling resentful and trapped. If we do not value our needs, then it is unlikely that anybody else will. If we do not know what they are, it is unlikely anyone else will figure that out for us. So, our needs go unmet and we begin to feel aggrieved about constantly giving everything of ourselves and leaving so much unsaid. But how do we get our message across, if our main aim is to please? We can – and do – repress or deny our emotions, but where do they go?

Over and above this, our partner may possibly be looking for more from a relationship than constant acquiescence – 'I don't mind, I'm happy to do what you want.' Making all the decisions can be tiring and sometimes our partner may just want us to pick the damn restaurant for once. Perhaps sometimes they want us to argue back when they are angry or not let them walk all over us. Although some people might find a certain satisfaction in continual dominance, many others may well prefer someone they can respect!

What we do is well-meaning and ultimately all we want is to be loved, but at the heart of it all is a belief that we have to be unselfish in order to get that love. We can often focus on constantly doing for others in order to get the payback of feeling needed. We can become over-involved in other people's lives and feel resentment when our partner wants to do things on their own. We may then resort to manipulation to get our emotional needs met, and have unrealistic expectations about what others should do for us. Expectations that are never voiced, of course. All of this can be very difficult for our partner to deal with.

What if our partner is not good for us and it would be in our best interests to leave the relationship? If our goal is to do anything to please, then as soon as the other person is not happy, we may have a problem. If we are with someone who takes advantage of our appeasing ways, and begins to try to control us or put us down, this can leave us feeling trapped and helpless.

If we cannot live with the guilt of telling someone we do not want to be with them anymore or we fear the repercussions, we may subconsciously decide to just put our heads down and accept our lot. 'It doesn't matter if they are controlling and put me down – they probably have their reasons. Maybe if I double my efforts to please them, I could turn this around and make them happy. Maybe this is all I deserve?'

It is this belief, that we are somehow not worthy of better or that others will leave us if we do not always put them first, that can cause us so much difficulty.

Turning the focus around

Relationships and emotions are difficult to navigate, so we need to know when we are making life harder than it needs to be. It's not easy to admit we are people-pleasers, and it's difficult to turn around a habit of a lifetime, but there are ways to start. We may need to work on our sense of worth and practise getting in touch with our own needs. We may also need to have an honest, hard look at why we do the things we do, whilst challenging some of our long-ingrained thought patterns around other people.

In starting to consider our own worth, it can be useful to ask ourselves why people are drawn to us. If we struggle with needing to please others, we are most probably generous, helpful and very considerate of others. Most importantly, we are likely to be extremely loving, and this can no doubt be felt by those who know us. There are, however, many other qualities that we no doubt have that are also highly valued by our loved ones. We need to look for times that we are appreciated or loved when we have done nothing, but just for who we are. Others may not always express their feelings in the way we are able to ourselves, but we have to learn to identify and acknowledge when those around us are showing us love.

Having said that, we also have to accept that we are perhaps not always the wonderful, loving, selfless person we see ourselves as! At least, that is not all we are. Nobody can be - it's just not humanly possible. We all have flaws and we need to be more accepting of them. It doesn't mean we will be rejected for them. In fact, it would be hard for our partners to live with someone who is perfect - especially if what has an outward face of perfection has an underbelly of resentment and manipulation. We have to be more conscious of our motives in doing what we do. If we were to have a truly honest look, we might see that some of our pleasing ways are done with the purpose of trying to get the other person to appreciate us and to meet our needs. Again, if we have wants and needs that are not explicitly spelled out, we are leaving ourselves open for disappointment, as the other person may not interpret our signals as we intended.

If people-pleasing is our habitual way of being, when trying to break out of it, we probably have to start small. If we are in a relationship, we could start making one choice or decision per week, no matter how uncomfortable (if we are not in a relationship, we can start this work with friends and family). We choose the movie, decide where we want to eat, what cereal to buy, where to shop, what to do one evening – it doesn't matter what it is, we just make one decision each week, based completely on our own inclinations, and suggest it to our partner.

We have to allow ourselves to feel out this process, especially since we may have real difficulties actually knowing what we do want. This doesn't matter: we still have to choose something. Note how it feels to make a decision. Note how it feels to tell your partner you want something. You have needs. Note what your brain is saying (spoiler – it won't be happy!). Anxiety Toolbox II (see page 94) will come in handy here.

Frame the situation – making a choice for yourself – in a Thought Record. Figure out what thoughts are coming up. Fears around feeling and being seen as selfish, how unfair you are being to your partner, and how unimpressed they will be, will be some common ones. We also need to acknowledge and move on from some of the most intrusive and persistent thoughts, such as, *They won't love me any more* or *It's selfish to put myself first*.

The more we can continue to ask ourselves what we want and force ourselves to make a choice, the more we begin to figure out what we actually do want. It's not about getting it right all the time, it's a process of discovery. As we go, we can step beyond what movie we want to watch, and move into the more important choices. We can still be generous, considerate and loving, whilst putting our own desires first from time to time. If we can learn to acknowledge and pursue our own needs, this will be a great addition to our loving nature. This nature will not go away if we look out for ourselves every once in a while.

Fear of conflict

There is probably nothing harder for a people-pleaser to navigate than an argument. Whether it is saying things we need to say when we are troubled by something in the relationship or defending ourselves when our partner is angry with us, this can be excruciating experience, as there will be a serious conflict of interest with our overall goal of keeping the other person happy.

In an intimate relationship, conflict is inevitable and crucial for the health of the relationship. Well, negotiation is the crucial element – but, more often than not, this plays out as conflict, as both parties do their best to navigate their way through the murky waters of undeclared feelings, unspoken expectations, misinterpretations and poor communication. This is not easy work, and we come up against the other person's expectations and needs at every turn, which often do not match our own. We have to be able to hear the other person, express our own needs clearly, compromise on areas where there is difference of opinion and, as best we can, allow both parties to sometimes do this poorly, especially in the early stages of the relationship.

If the thought of an argument fills us with dread,

chances are we will have avoided them all our lives. If this is the case, we will be more inclined to withdraw from conflict or only face up to it under great duress, rather than seeing it as an opportunity to say our piece, hear what the other person has to say and then jointly figure out what needs to be done to proceed. If we have always avoided difficult conversations, we may have poor negotiation skills or we may harbour unhelpful beliefs that we will not be listened to or rejected if we put forward our own needs.

Anything for an easy life

With anxiety, we can often long for the easy life. We want things to be comfortable and predictable, with little uncertainty, everything within our control and as little conflict as possible. Unfortunately, this kind of life does not exist, especially if we are to share it with another human being.

Like so many coping mechanisms that are designed to avoid things we find frightening, seeking comfort over conflict is counterproductive. If, for example, we use distractions such as social media or daydreaming to give us respite from the anxiety of a big project at work, this may give us momentary relief – but the project won't progress or have much chance of success. Likewise, constantly avoiding conflict in a relationship can push the awkward conversation down the road a little, but the conversation still needs to be had, and the likelihood is that, when we finally get around to it, it's a much, much more difficult conversation than it originally needed to be.

The bottom line is that the anything-for-an-easy-life approach to a relationship can leave us with anything but an easy life! Short-term avoidance of pain is very seductive if the quiet life is our goal, but, in the long run, it just paves the way for much greater suffering further down the road. If a lot of conversations we have with our partner involve some sort of mental gymnastics on our part, where we are trying to figure out the best thing to say so as not to bring on conflict, then this can come back to bite us very quickly.

The best thing about the truth, as Mark Twain put it, is that you don't need to remember anything. If we lie to avoid conflict or to protect the other person's feelings, those lies are now out in the world and may haunt us.

I can remember a perfect example of this from my own life, when I was in my mid-twenties. I was out one afternoon and bumped into an ex-girlfriend, and we ended up having a coffee. The relationship had not ended well, and the two hours we spent talking seemed to be quite healing for both of us. Later that day, when I met up with my then current girlfriend and she asked me how my day went, I, in my wisdom, decided not to mention the two hours with my ex.

I remember my thoughts clearly. I wanted to protect my girlfriend's feelings, and I also wanted to avoid a conflict. Two days later, we bumped into a mutual friend who knew both my ex and my current girlfriend. During the course of a quick chat, he remarked, 'I hear you met X the other day.' My girlfriend looked at me and said nothing, but I knew there would most definitely be a conversation coming when we were alone – and how do you imagine my lie by omission looked now? A quick explanation when she first asked me about my day would have been easy and something she could have handled. Her feelings did not need protecting. But now this had become something that could not be so easily explained away!

What happened next – and this was very much the way I would have dealt with such situations in the past – was that I tried to explain to my then current girlfriend my reasoning for what I had done, gradually drip-feeding small increments of the truth as I went. I was on the defensive and my goal was still to above all avoid conflict – regardless of the fact that I was already in the middle of a conflict! So, instead of addressing things head-on and having it out fully – remember, I hadn't actually done anything wrong other than not mention the meeting with my ex – I got things to a place where my girlfriend and I were no longer fighting and then I just waited it out until everything seemed OK again.

It may sound like a crazy way to operate but, in my mid-twenties, I had nothing else at my disposal when handling such situations. It was how I had dealt with things since I was a child, when it actually served me quite well. I even didn't realise at the time that I was falling back on a maladaptive defence mechanism that, apart from anything else, was no longer appropriate to my situation as an adult, when my environment had changed and I was interacting with people beyond the family circle. It's what I had always done, and I had no awareness that it wasn't an optimal way of operating, that there were other, better approaches I could have used or that other people don't need protecting from the truth.

This is just one small example of how opting for the easy life can be counterproductive - but this principle can and does play out like this to varying degrees in most of our lives. It can drive a partner crazy if we are constantly looking to appease them, rather than really engaging and saying what we truly think and feel. This approach can leave us scrambling around in our heads, searching furiously for a way out of a stupid, insignificant lie we told yesterday, just so that things will be OK. And the annoying thing is that the silly lie was so unnecessary in the first place. Although there was no malice in it - it was just something we concocted to avoid a potential argument - the end result was still needless upset and pain for our partner and ourselves.

Another thing to also be conscious of if we never engage in conflict is the question of what we do with the anger or hurt we feel but which we don't act on. Chances are our true feelings will come out in other ways, and we may punish the other person through jokes, snide remarks, silence or passive-aggressive behaviour. It is a way to try to get our point across whilst still not engaging in an open and honest conversation. This can be a frustrating and confusing form of communication for the other person to deal with. We're expecting them to pick up on our signals and know why we are sending them, whilst not acknowledging them ourselves.

This refusal to engage can also be used as a way to take away our partner's right to call us out in the relationship. If on another occasion, they get annoyed and bring up things that are bothering them, we can use the fact that we never complain about all their failings to shame them into silence. We can make it look like everything would be perfect if only they weren't so disagreeable – when in fact they are most likely well within their rights to mention their dissatisfaction sometimes. Because *sometimes* is more often than *never*, it looks like they do all the complaining, making them the bad guys.

Build and explode

Another common way those who cannot abide conflict try to get their needs met whilst avoiding an argument is to let things slide for a long time until the pressure builds and it is suddenly released in an outpouring of anger. The sins of the previous months are brought to the table with such force that the other person does not know what has hit them.

If this is the way we handle conflict, then there is a pretty reliable pattern to our disagreements. Something happens that bothers us, perhaps small enough, but we let it slide. Maybe we go quiet or are 'off' for the day, but if the other person asks us about it, we will say that nothing is wrong. Slowly, the annoyance passes, and things get back to normal – but we haven't forgotten. Every minute detail is stored in our memory. Soon enough, something else occurs that we are not happy with and, again, we say nothing, choosing instead to simply shut down as before. We are not comfortable saying that we find something our partner has done annoys us - but the rising tide of anger will soon override this discomfort! When it finally comes - maybe one, maybe ten more incidents further down the road - the anger trumps the fear of conflict or any other barriers to discussion.

We blurt out everything that has been bothering us. We drag up the past and talk about things that we have been stewing over for a long time, with little regard for the fact that our partner may be hearing all this for the first time and now has to come up with a rebuttal while wondering what the hell has just happened. We trample over the feelings of the other person and say things that are designed to hurt because, after all, we have been hurting for a long time.

At the heart of this very damaging pattern is the fact that, in order to finally address the issues that are bothering us, we have to be in such a state of heightened emotion, that we are neither in full control of what we say nor are we able to listen to and digest what the other person is saying. In order to see the other person's point of view, we have to come down from the anger - yet we cannot come down from our anger because, if we do so, we will land in our fear of conflict.

These sudden explosions of anger can leave us, and of course our partners, shell-shocked after the event. We might not recognise the person we become in that moment and deeply regret some of the things we say or how we make our partner feel. We may feel helpless that this is our only form of getting what we want or we may have misplaced anger towards our partner, blaming them for bringing out this response in us. There can be so much inner turmoil because, after the anger dies down, the very beliefs and fears that stopped us talking in the beginning still remain. Our heightened anxiety now churns away in hindsight, working through everything that happened after the anger and outrage took over.

Communication is key

If you recognise yourself in any of the conflict avoidance styles mentioned above, all of which are unproductive and deeply damaging to a relationship, it is probably time to look at a different approach. We all know that good communication is crucial. If done well, it can allow a relationship to become a sanctuary against the world – a place where you can show your real self, be vulnerable, feel acceptance, and also be strong and supportive.

But what if the idea of open and honest communication terrifies us? As with all fears, when our brain fires a 'danger' thought at us and we react in a way that confirms the danger – in this case, not engaging in difficult conversations – the fear grows. If we have practised avoiding conflict for a very long time, we can be sure the fear is fairly well-established. This is likely an area where we are going to have to change the way we behave in order to prove to our brains that we no longer find conflict as frightening.

To begin the process of change, we will have to push through some seriously negative thoughts that will be telling us to run. Much like with the work we did earlier with uncertainty, we need to work on building a tolerance for conflict, and this will take time. That's one of the main difficulties with this kind of work. It will not be all plain sailing and big achievements. It may be slow and feel awkward, and we will have to push through some of our fears.

Say, for example, we have a fear of losing the other person, so we keep our head in the sand and ignore all the things that bother us. If we lift our heads up and really engage and tell the other person what we want and don't want, there is a chance we will find out that our partner is not capable of meeting our needs. That isn't a great realisation to have to face – but what are the alternatives? We can continue in the same way, with our needs being neglected, hoping that one day things will change. But why would they? If our partner is not getting feedback when things are bothering us, it is not beyond the realm of possibility that they might believe everything is OK. It is time to start taking responsibility for our own needs and, with our partner, negotiate how we can have them met.

Importantly, this process is best engaged in after we have done some of the work on our sensitivity levels as outlined on pages 201-3. Then, we decide that, the next time we feel we need to stick up for ourselves or point out something that is bothering us in the relationship, we will, to the best of our ability, address this directly with our partner. During this exchange, we have to allow for two things. We have to accept that we may go about the task clumsily and with little polish at first – if we have been avoiding this all our lives, there will be a steep learning curve involved – and we also must allow the other person time to process the message.

This new approach from us will likely also be new for our partner – especially if we have been with them for a long time. We have to allow them their in-the-moment response, which may involve confusion, anger or any other range of emotions as they gather their thoughts. But we must also allow them time to go away and process what has been said. We cannot judge the outcome of this first sortie into conflict by the immediate response of our partner.

If we don't jump to conclusions that what's happening in the moment is indicative of what's actually going to happen in the longer term, it is much easier to stay calm. What we experience in the moment, how it feels ('they don't care about me', 'they don't listen to what I say', and so on), may not actually be what is going on. Admittedly, it's hard to do this at the time of the argument, but later, on reflection, we can soften the situation for ourselves, as we allow the other person to process what has been said. We can then use this evidence to gain composure in future disagreements. This is where using the strategy (from Anxiety Toolbox I, see page 65), of zooming out on the timeline can be so helpful, allowing us the perspective and calm to see that another conversation may be needed when both parties have processed the other's position.

When we decide to speak up, we need to say what it is that we are not satisfied with, expect the other person to push back and try as best we can to stick to the point we want to make. We need to let go of the outcome in the short term.

When enough time has passed, we can think about the beliefs we went into the situation with and how accurate they were. What did we believe would happen if we pointed out something in the relationship that we were not happy about? This can be a great time to do a really detailed Thought Record (see page 98) about what actually did happen, to bring some balance and perspective and calm our worried mind, and challenge the hypotheses our fears have had us believing in for so long.

Finally, it's important for us to know that there is most likely no magical place we can get to in our minds where we will be totally fine with conflict. From my own experience, I can say that I have been working on my own difficulties in this area for a long time, and it remains something I have to really stay on top of. My thoughts are exactly the same as they always were - *Don't say that. Just do this instead. Let that slide, it doesn't really matter. Just walk away; be the bigger person.* However, such thoughts have become quieter and less persistent.

My mind still immediately says 'avoid', when I'm presented with an opportunity either to take part in a disagreement or find a way around it, but it's much easier to push past this way of thinking because, by now, I have done it many times before and my brain no longer sees ignoring such thoughts as potentially dangerous and unwise. However, even now, while I know full well that honest, direct communication is the only way forward, if I am not vigilant, I can still find myself shying away from it.

I've come to realise that, when it comes to situations of conflict, my thoughts can still be sneaky. I pride myself on being calm and composed, but this can often be used by my brain as an excuse to hold back and not engage. If I listened to my oft-ignored gut, I would be involved in many more disagreements, but my head keeps telling me it's better to leave things alone. But I have now recognised and accepted this in myself, which makes it easier to catch and push through the thoughts, and I'm able to do this so much more than I used to.

That's all I can ask of myself really. Am I better at this than I was yesterday? Marginally. But if I can say that every day, that's real progress.

Chapter 12
Anxiety Toolbox IV

In Chapters 4, 6 and 9, the first three parts of the Anxiety Toolbox, we have looked at a number of tools and concrete strategies designed to help us begin to engage with our thoughts in a different way, so that we gradually gain greater control over anxiety. As we progress through the initial stages, it is very important to keep pushing on with our lives, cutting ourselves a break when we need to and learning to accept that we will not always be progressing. If we can continue to move on with our lives as a parallel process to the ongoing work on our anxiety, we will be more easily able to see that anxiety is just one aspect of our being and not the all-encompassing monster that we can often make it out to be.

In this chapter, we will be looking at broader approaches and strategies in which we can engage to enhance our lives in a more general way, which in turn will help loosen the hold worry and anxiety have over us.

Working towards our best selves: a method from Brief Therapy

A key strategy that really seems to help with anxiety management in a general way is to start doing again the things that worry or low mood have taken away from us over the years. It's a process we should try to engage in alongside the work we are doing directly with anxiety: we don't want to have to wait for that work to be completed before we begin claiming back the aspects of our lives that have fallen away because of our fears or try new things we want to do but which anxiety held us back from.

One way of giving some helpful structure to this process is to use a method from Brief Therapy (a short-term, solution-focused form of therapy), which involves drawing on what we already know about ourselves from a time in the past when we found life easier.

The idea is to take a simple scale of one to ten, and plot our way up that scale towards an 'ideal' version of ourselves. First, we need to get a strong, concrete idea of what a ten would look like. This can be a version of ourselves when we were at our best – perhaps from a certain time in our youth or in college or during a summer away or any time when we did not feel that worry or our anxiety was such a big deal – no matter how brief or fleeting that period was. We need to really try to remember that time and pin down some details for ourselves. What were we like? What were we doing? How were we interacting with other people? What was different about us to how we are now?

If you can't think of any time like this, do you have a vision of how you would like to be in the future, if anxiety was less of a problem? If such a vision doesn't immediately come to mind, you may need to indulge in a bit of fantasy and turn off the cynical side of your brain! Imagine you go to sleep one night and, as you are sleeping, a miracle happens. When you wake up in the morning, your anxiety and intrusive thoughts have completely gone. You no longer know how to worry and you cannot relearn it. Your mind has stopped firing negative thoughts at you; things you once found frightening no longer scare you. So, now try to pin down what differences you would notice in yourself and in how you would interact with others. What would your loved ones notice about you that was different? What would you be doing that you do not do now – in your relationships, at work and in your free time? Really try to flesh out the picture.

When we've done this preparation, we will go on to rate ourselves against our ideal. So, if ten is us at our absolute best, where are we now?

Using the scale in this way serves two purposes. Firstly, it gives us a sense of how far from our best selves we think we are. If we feel we are a four, OK, that's below halfway, but it's not as low as it could be. If it's a two, then we know we have some work to do, but we have a good sense of where we are and where we would like to get to. The rating process also gives us a starting point and a more tangible feel of what we are working towards.

So, let's say we think we are a three. Our overall goal is ten but, for now, let's not worry too much about whether we get there or not. For now, we are going to shrink the timeframe right down and aim for four. We have looked at what a ten is, and we know how we feel now, so, using our imagination, can we think about what just one rung up the ladder would look like? Can we flesh out a four? We're not looking for massive change here, we are just aiming up and looking to start moving forward in small increments.

So, if we were a four, what would we be doing that we are not doing now? Out walking more perhaps? Asking a friend out for coffee or lunch? Would we be spending less time on social media, eating a proper breakfast, looking after ourselves a little better generally? Keep it simple but identify two or three concrete things that you could start doing, regardless of the objections from your brain, in the spirit of getting yourself galvanised into action and moving forwards.

As we're able to tick those initial few things off our list, we keep fleshing out a four and doing the things that that version of ourselves would be doing. Then we turn our attention to five and what that would look like. And so it continues.

Let the work we are doing on our anxiety be one thing and this push towards our better selves be another. The two processes will feed into one another, and at times overlap, but it is always better not to wait until we are feeling better to start moving in a positive direction. It is in action that we get motivation, and it is as our brain observes us voluntarily facing our fears and expanding our lives that it will gradually stop sending the warning signals of anxiety and worry, and this, in turn, enables our confidence to grow.

Drop the comparison habit

Constantly comparing ourselves to others is a fantastic way to ramp up anxiety and feelings of not being good enough. We do it all the time. We look at others on social media, with their seemingly perfect lives, and we feel bad about our own mundane existence. We walk by people on the street and think that we are not as fit, good-looking, well-dressed, and so on. We look at our friends, colleagues, celebrities – whoever is at hand – and decide we don't measure up. None of this is helped by the fact that all we can see is our own weaknesses and everyone else's strengths.

Take the example of comparing ourselves with regard to work and our career. There are two main ways in which this tends to play out in relation to the working world. Firstly, we look to our friends and peers who we qualified or finished college with – acquaintances, cousins, neighbours, anyone of roughly our own age, people we knew before we all started our careers. We look at their job titles, who they work for or where they are on the career ladder, and we begin to feel that we are not doing as well or are falling behind. Of course, we ignore those who don't seem to be doing as well as we are. They don't seem to count, for some reason!

As so often happens with worry and anxiety, we allow ourselves to get wound up emotionally about a situation without taking the full set of facts into account. We look at others, make presumptions and jump to conclusions, yet frequently we really only have basic information about them.

We do not know what part luck or connections have had in their apparent ascent. We have no idea how they see their own progress or how they compare themselves to us. We don't know what levels of stress they may be under or what they have had to sacrifice to get to where they are. We don't have a clue as to whether they are actually happy or have any degree of contentment in their lives. All we can see is that they are there and we are here - and that here is not good enough, and we are going to make it mean all sorts of bad things about ourselves, both now and in the future (thanks, Brain!).

One thing that we can probably accurately assume is that, if they did not have the handicap of worry and anxiety to contend with, there were certain roadblocks and obstacles that they did not have to overcome. If they did have difficulties with their thoughts, perhaps they had better coping skills to manage their anxiety. We looked earlier at the damage anxiety can do to a career - the wish to stay in our comfort zone, seeking out only things that are safe. The struggle to deal with uncertainty in a complex environment. Climbing the career ladder when you are constantly worried can be like running a 100-metre race while dragging a bag of sand behind you. You can make progress, but every metre is hard-won.

Building a satisfying and meaningful life is, however, a longer-term venture that can take many different turns and generally consists of many different aspects beyond just a successful career – such as developing quality relationships with family and friends, identifying a value system that sits well with who we are, developing our spirituality and fulfilling our creative potential, and so on. In all of these areas, as in our professional lives, as we learn to become more aware of what is holding us back, figure out how best to move forward and face some of the fears we have otherwise turned away from, we can begin to make bigger strides and experience a greater degree of personal growth.

In our working lives, the other group of people we constantly compare ourselves with are those with whom we work directly. On the face of it, there is nothing wrong with this one. Evaluating our peers and seeing how we stack up alongside them can act as a good barometer. It can show us our strengths, but also where we might need to improve. In the right circumstances, it can spur us on to greater things. The ability to compare ourselves accurately with others can therefore be a good tool. However, the problem with anxiety, negative thinking, social anxiety and worry is that they make comparing ourselves accurately with others impossible. This is because very often our starting point is the belief that others are better than us in every way – more intelligent, more competent, funnier, more interesting and more socially adjusted. They find life easier, have fewer problems and, generally, they are opposite of us – they are 'normal'.

This comparison cannot go well for us. There can only be one winner. We don't do a critical analysis of our colleagues, looking at their strengths and weaknesses to determine where and how they could improve or where they could be stronger. Throw into the mix the fact that those prone to anxiety tend to downplay their accomplishments, strengths and abilities. Until we can properly acknowledge these, let's just stop the comparisons! In Chapters 7 and 8 (Anxiety in the Workplace – Parts One and Two), we looked at how we can work to combat the negative thinking patterns that can undermine us at work. And dropping the need to compare is one very important step in the right direction.

Now, have a think about this. There will be people out there who will look at us and think, 'God, I wish I was as together as they are!' Everyone else just sees the things we say and do. They do not have access to our journey or all the things that are going on in our heads. They do not know what scares us or how difficult we find things. They just see the end product, and they, like us, compare themselves without all the information. That's how little idea any of us has about what is going on for other people. And that's how crazy this need to compare is!

One step forward: how to deal with the inevitable sense of going backwards

We all have an idea of how life should be going, and how things should be working out for us: *If I do this, then that should happen. If I follow this path, then I will get these results.* We may not have it all explicitly thought out, but we know what feels like progress, and we certainly notice when we sense that we're going in the other direction. When we first decide it is time to tackle the problem of anxiety, we may not know exactly how to go about it at the beginning, but we definitely know that we want to feel better. What is certainly not in the plan is feeling better for a short time and then going back to feeling exactly the way we did before.

The feeling of being back at square one is such a common theme in all types of personal development work that is dealt with as a specific issue in therapy. We go to a therapist looking for help and start working towards making things better. We gain some early ground, facing fears and feeling good about our progress. Our confidence is a little higher and we feel as if things are beginning to change – and then we are hit with something that knocks us sideways. It may be something we've addressed already, something we thought we were 'over', or an event that suddenly brings back the old feelings of fear, failure, inadequacy, low mood, helplessness or whatever other horribly familiar feeling it is that screams, 'You haven't changed!'

When my clients come back to me in these

circumstances, there is often a feeling of the air being sucked out of the room. They will express a great sense of despondency, that the old ways of feeling and responding to anxiety seem to have returned. There can also be some embarrassment from them, that we might now have to go back over old ground, areas that they 'should' be on top of already.

One of the most important parts of tackling and managing anxiety, especially in the early stages, is learning to manage the periods when we feel we are stuck or there is a sense of regression. Perspective, above all else, is crucial in these moments. We need to step back from the feelings and look at the bigger picture.

Often, when we feel like we are back at square one, we have shrunk our timeframe to incorporate only the immediate period we are in. We lose sight of the gains we have made and the previous times when we tackled similar issues successfully. If we look only at the day on which things have been difficult, we will draw a certain conclusion. If we broaden the timeline to take in, say, the previous week, we may see a more balanced picture. If we go out to a month and take in some of the big wins we have had, this recent setback may now only seem like a blip. The most important thing is what we do from here. Do we pack it all in or do we continue as we were when things were going well?

As we have discussed throughout this book, when it comes to anxiety, most of us have spent years learning to think the way we think, react the way we react and feel the way we feel. A lot of our coping mechanisms were developed at an early age, when they made perfect sense for the environment we were in. When we grow up, however, and our environment changes, we do not realise we still have some maladaptive coping mechanisms that no longer fit our new reality. As we learn new tools and begin to change the way we interact with anxiety, it is only natural that we will be met with some pushback from our older, established ways of being. *You always ran from anxiety – what are you doing now, facing it head-on? You always got caught up in your negative thoughts – but now you think paying less attention to them is the way to go?*

In therapy, we often go back over the same ground again and again, each time gaining new insights and a greater sense of control. In times of regression, we need to bring in compassion and curiosity. We need to acknowledge that this work is tough, allow ourselves to make mistakes and to fall back into old patterns of behaviour sometimes and be genuinely curious about the way things are shaping up for us.

How do we best judge our progress?

If we feel that our progress is not as it should be, one question we might ask ourselves is, 'Am I consistently putting in the work I need to, to be able to keep on top of my anxiety?' As I've mentioned, if someone comes to me for therapy, and that is the only hour in the week in which they are working on their mental health, then it will be very hard for them to make progress. No matter how much our anxiety is playing up, we have, as we have seen throughout this book, choices in how we respond. We may need to review the work we are putting in and decide if it is sufficient to tackle what we are dealing with.

If we really believe we are putting in the work but we're still experiencing setbacks (which are, as we have said, inevitable), then we may need to manage our expectations. If we are looking for immediate results or continual, visible progress, we may be disappointed and feel as if we are going nowhere fast. This goes back again to the concept of mastery from Anxiety Toolbox I (see page 54), where we spoke about how very easy it can be to mistake a plateau for a setback. We need to become more comfortable on the plateau, just doing the work needed that will enable us both to tolerate and manage our anxiety.

We may only be getting short bursts of progress followed by long periods of plateauing, but the current plateau is most likely higher on the curve towards mastery than the previous one, so there *is* real progress there, it's just that it's hard to quantify. Take the scenario, where there's a baby in your extended family that you only see every three months or so – each time you see them, you are amazed at how fast they have grown and what progress they have made. For the parents, who are with the child every day, the child's growth is not so obvious.

This is similar to what happens for us as we learn to managing anxiety over time. Because we are within our own heads all the time and we have to deal with our anxiety on a constant basis, it is hard to believe we are making real progress. We do not notice how much we have grown, and we lose sight of where we were. Things that used to cause us high anxiety, we are now able to manage to a tolerable level, so we no longer think about how hard it was for us. It is great that things are no longer as difficult, but we can easily lose perspective.

This is particularly true if we are using our feelings as a barometer for how we are doing. Feelings are not facts. We still *feel* anxious, so we presume things are not going well. What we need is a better way to measure our progress, whilst learning to tolerate difficult emotions. We have to learn to expand the timeframe, and look at the week or month or year and not just the uncomfortable feeling of setback we are dealing with today.

Changing our mindset

Sometimes, it is a change in mindset or a different way of looking at things that helps. To begin with, we cannot have regressed if we have not first progressed. So, we can see that a backwards step is actually evidence of progress, rather than proof that we will never get anywhere or that we have somehow failed. It's just part of the process. If we have progressed before, we can and will again.

A step backwards absolutely does not mean we are back to square one. A regression does not mean we lose all the awareness we have built up or the new knowledge and coping skills we have acquired. We are still armed with the tools that will enable us to move forward and put the blip behind us.

Another example of how we frame things to ourselves is to change the language we use when talking about the days or weeks when it feels that things are not going as well as we would like – and indeed the times when they are going better than we expected.

Language is important. If you say, 'I had a bad week because I was anxious', it will give you a sense of helplessness when your anxiety strikes. If, instead, you say, 'I didn't have a good week, because I didn't manage my anxiety as well as I might have', and you can acknowledge areas for learning, it gives you a greater sense of control over, and indeed responsibility for, your own mental health.

Likewise, if you have a good week, it's most helpful if you can look at it from the perspective of what you did to manage your mood and define more clearly why the week was good. So, rather than saying, 'I didn't feel too much anxiety this week', you might be more precise and frame it differently by saying, 'I listened to my body this week and addressed my anxious thoughts early. I exercised three times and I talked with my partner about something that was bothering me.' This makes things clearer and, again, gives you back more control over what happened, rather than seeing yourself as a leaf in the air, at the mercy of the ever-changing winds!

Ultimately, as we do this work, we must never lose focus of the reasons we decided to tackle anxiety in the first place. What has it taken from our lives? How has it affected our career, our relationships, our peace of mind and our motivation? Where would we be if we just left it unchecked and carried on as before? When we keep bringing ourselves back to our 'why', we will find it easier to stick with the work we are doing and see it as a life-long process rather merely than a quick, limited fix.

Chapter 13
Escape

Not so long ago, I spent a year writing articles about anxiety. I started a website with a blog, and away I went. I knew that in the initial stages of blogging, your readership stats tend to be very low, because no one knows yet that you exist, so I decided to learn a little about online marketing and some of the dos and don'ts of starting a blog and building a following.

One of the main things you need is content, and lots of it. This was of course not a shock to me, as I knew I would have to get busy, and that was fine. What I found striking, though, was the kind of language that was being recommended in order to attract more readers – and this was especially true as regards the titles of the articles or blog entries. I learned that there were seven key words or phrases that would invariably draw a reader in, and that it was a good idea to use at least one of them in the title of every article. They are as follows:

1. Today

2. Right now

3. Fast

4. Works quickly

5. Step-by-step

6. Easy

7. Quick

8. Simple

If I was to talk about my own journey through anxiety – and where I am now versus where I began – none of the words or phrases on the above list would enter into the conversation. I'm sure there are quick ways to fix a leaky tap or step-by-step guides that can help you prepare the perfect meal, but getting on top of and managing our anxiety doesn't work that way.

There is no doubt that when we are in pain, physical or emotional, we want the fix to be quick and effective. If we have a low tolerance for certain emotions – like anger, fear and sadness – we may seek to change these emotions as quickly as possible. So, we reach for the quick fix, and there are plenty out there, including alcohol, drugs, porn and food. We can use these to change a mood we cannot tolerate or relieve a pain we cannot bear.

The quick fix is so seductive because it appears to work. It offers us a break from the intolerable feelings and, initially, can seem like a great way to cope with strong emotions. It is, however, a very short-term solution, and one which often causes more harm than good in the medium to long term.

If, for example, we use alcohol to take the edge off our anxiety on a work night, we may end up drinking too much, sleeping poorly, and waking up late and hungover. If this becomes our coping mechanism of choice, it's not difficult to predict the consequences. Soon the effect of the quick fix is not as intense or as long-lasting as it first was, and we need to drink more to achieve the same level of cut-off. As this escalates, it is clear that far greater emotional turmoil will be waiting for us a little further down the road.

Finding a better way to deal with these emotions is not only difficult, it requires ongoing diligence on our parts and the hard work of building the new approach into our lives. Along with learning how to manage our anxiety, we also have to unlearn all the maladaptive coping mechanisms that we have relied on through the years. Not only will we come up against our overriding desire for the easiest and most familiar option time after time, but our inner voice will be telling us our new strategy isn't working, that it's too difficult and that we should just fall back into our old ways of coping. After all, they have worked for us well enough until now – and all this awareness nonsense is overrated anyway.

Uncomfortably numb

When anxiety is a long-term fixture in our lives, we may go through periods where we are coping well and feeling good, only for these to be followed by a bout of feeling anxious again. We struggle with being able to define the source of our anxiety, but we are also unsure of why we were happy during the better times.

To not feel anxious any more is our most pressing goal, and so we self-medicate with escape. The longer this pattern continues, the more escape becomes something we just do anyway, regardless of how we are feeling. It can leave us feeling numb a lot of the time, since our escape mechanisms take the edge off all our emotions, not just the 'bad' ones. However numb is better than anxious, and so we keep on repeating the same behaviours.

There is an endless list of things we can use for escape purposes. Anything that is powerful enough to change our mood or relieve our pain will suffice. Alcohol, porn, social media, drugs, computer games, shopping, eating, binge-watching online videos or TV shows, always keeping busy – these can all take our anxiety away momentarily. They all work, and work really well, in the short term. They are not necessarily all problematic of course. A glass of wine with dinner can be great, whereas opening a bottle each night with a view to having one or two glasses and then, more often than not, finishing the lot might be something we want to have a think about. Similarly, unwinding with computer games can be a fun pastime, but playing all night and not getting enough sleep before work might need addressing.

We really need to look at how an activity is affecting our lives to decide if it is a problem or a pastime. We must step back and examine why we are doing what we are doing. Do we have control over when, for how long and how frequently we engage? If we realise an activity is having an obviously negative impact on our lives, are we able to stop? Is our engagement in the behaviour having an effect on our relationships? Answering these questions will give us a better idea of how much of an issue or not an activity is for us.

We can use most innocuous things to escape our thoughts and emotions, if they work. But the problem is not the activity in itself – it's the extent to which we rely on it to avoid aspects of reality.

To take an example from my own life: as a child, I was a great daydreamer. It began with not knowing how to handle difficult situations and emotions, meaning that I would escape into a fantasy world in my own head. Very quickly, though, I began to daydream all the time. My teachers saw it as an inability to concentrate and I was often described as lazy or having my head 'in the clouds'.

In my teens, when I began to develop my own taste in music, daydreaming and music became an intoxicating combination for me, especially when it came to what I would regard as meaningful and melancholic music. I could play certain songs and be immediately removed from my reality – and, more importantly, my emotions.

Again, this is what we all use music for to some extent, and there's nothing wrong with that in itself. If, however, we are using it constantly to remove ourselves from the present and cannot stop doing it, even though our studying, work, sleep and human interactions are being affected, then this is something different.

In my case, I could be in a group of people at a social event or in a work meeting or even in a one-on-one conversation but, in my mind, I was off somewhere else entirely, many miles away in my own fantasy world. You may laugh and think, 'Big deal!', but when I look back on my twenties, I realise now the extent to which it had become such a habit, my way of escaping anxiety, that I'm not sure how much time I spent in the real world.

Today, I use mindfulness techniques – such as those we looked at in Chapter 9 (Anxiety Toolbox III) – to both catch myself when I'm wandering off into my thoughts or daydreams, and to bring myself back to the present each time. My point here is that even now (I'm forty-two at the time of writing), my tendency to escape into daydreams is still something I need to be aware of constantly. It is such an effective short-term coping mechanism that I developed at such an early age that I figure it will always be something I have to keep on top of.

In my work with clients over the past number of years, I have found that social media and pornography are increasingly powerful and problematic escape methods that people really struggle with. I work with a lot of young professionals, and while alcohol and drugs, problematic eating, computer game overuse, and shopping/overspending are up there in terms of common maladaptive methods of escape, it is social media and porn overuse, above all, that seem to be the most widespread, most accessible and most insidious (as, mostly, they are not viewed as inherently problematic activities). And so, I am going to look at each in some detail in the rest of this chapter.

Social media

Like many of the activities we use as escapism, there is nothing wrong with social media per se, it's how we engage with it that can be problematic. If we are lost in an online world for long periods of the day and social media is the first thing we check in the morning and the last thing we look at before we go to sleep, we may need to examine our usage. If we often make it a priority over our real-life relationships, we need to give some thought to how it is serving us. One of the things that makes the social-media compulsion even more difficult to kick is that even when we are not actively engaged with it, it is constantly soliciting our attention. A message, an image, an update, a comment, a 'like' – all of these are heralded by an alert, letting us know something has 'happened', and that we need to check back in.

This constant engagement removes us from the world around us and robs us of time with our partner, family or friends. I have often counselled clients who feel they have almost completely lost their partners to social media. They feel like they cannot compete and even after conversations around usage, their partner will quickly slip back into old ways. This continued overusage, even in the face of evidence that the relationship is being damaged, would suggest there is more than simple enjoyment at play.

Social media is, of course, a blessing as well as a curse. It's how we can keep in touch with friends and gain new knowledge. It's often how we discover communities of people with whom we share similarities, and who we might not have found in our own physical world. It's also increasingly where we find love, sex, friendships, new music, teachers, mentors and, generally, sources of inspiration. However, we do need to find balance, and learn to recognise when we are using the online world as an escape from our thoughts and feelings. While it can be good to get away from ourselves and reality from time to time, we have to be able to recognise when we are no longer in control of when and for how long we engage, and acknowledge what we might be neglecting whilst we are 'away'.

It's also really important to be aware that, although we might be seeking escape from certain difficult feelings and truths when we spend long periods on social media, it can often be the case that the pain we experience whilst engaging is worse than what we are running from. There are many aspects of social media that can feed into our anxiety or have a negative effect on our mental health. Although there are certainly more than these three areas of difficulty, it is the anxiety around engagement, the constant, implied comparison between ourselves and others, and the draw of heated discussions on topics that may run contrary to our values and beliefs that most commonly come up as problematic for my clients.

Rules of engagement in the world of social media

If we are using our real identity on social media – as opposed to being there anonymously under a random username – many of the same issues and rules we live with in real life will follow us online. The anxieties we have around real-life social situations and human interactions will still apply. People-pleasing, fear of conflict, intolerance of uncertainty (for example, what people think of us, what they meant by a comment or by their lack of comment), and so on, will all play out online as they do in real life. The only difference – and it is a crucial one – is that with social media, we cannot go to our rooms and lock the world out, as we always bring the world everywhere with us. We may feel we can never get away from our online world, and therefore our anxieties and worries around our human interactions there are ever-present. We could do with a break from time to time!

When we engage with social media, we are not just talking to one person: we are talking to a much wider audience, and this is what can make it so much more anxiety-inducing – we can feel that there is so much more at stake. When we put something out there, the wait to see how many people will like or comment on it can be full of nervous anticipation. We worry about how we are being perceived and whether what we have said might cause offence or make us look stupid. We overthink what it means if our comments are not replied to, our pictures are not liked or we are not included in pictures posted by others in our social network. Everything we put out there gets amplified. And, online, we can be attacked or judged by the group in a way that would not happen in real life.

Just because we are not with other people does not mean we cannot be humiliated and feel judged. If we are socially anxious, we will feel the same sense of reticence online as in real life. We will adopt safety behaviours there too, such as limiting our interaction to comments of support or approval of others, if we comment at all, that is. We may put something out there that we think is funny, only to delete it a short time later after our brain tells us it might not be as funny as we thought, and that people will think we're weird. Approaching someone on dating app will fill us with the same sense of trepidation and overwhelming fear of rejection that we feel in a bar on a night out.

Comparisons

In Chapter 12 (Anxiety Toolbox – Part IV), we looked at the drawbacks of constantly comparing ourselves with others. This issue is particularly acute when it comes to social media. Two of the main problematic areas in the online world tend to be comparing our lives with the online version of the lives of our friends, and measuring ourselves up against the airbrushed images and lifestyles of the 'professionally beautiful'.

For those of us who struggle with self-confidence and self-worth, being able to have constant access to the online version of our friends' lives can be undermining and misery-inducing, particularly as what is being projected there is very rarely 100 per cent accurate. We are to a large extent comparing ourselves to a fantasy. The pictures may be real, but they have been carefully selected and perhaps edited, and they are not a full representation of the person's life. Our real lives can only feel boring or insignificant in comparison. If we were to compare our 'edited highlights' with what we see on other people's social media pages, that might be a more accurate comparison, but it might still not be comparing like for like. As well as this, it seems that only a certain type of personality is favoured on social media, and if we don't conform to that, we may well feel in some way inadequate. We may be more introverted and value more time by ourselves, we may have different interests, needs and wants unique to ourselves – but if everyone else's online persona is a fun-loving, outgoing party animal, it may be hard to compare ourselves positively.

When it comes to what I call the 'professionally beautiful' – those whose full-time job it is to look amazing and have wonderful, exciting lives, every detail of which they share online – we are on a highway to nothing. Perfect lives, perfect finances, perfect eating, perfect bodies. How are we meant to measure up? How does our life look in comparison?

Again, there is nothing wrong with these people or this lifestyle per se – it is our response to and interaction with them that may be having a damaging effect on our mental health. If we are following the beautiful people for motivation and inspiration, in our drive to be fitter, eat more healthily and generally become better versions of ourselves, then great. If, however, all our engagement with their online lives does is to make us feel inadequate and bad about ourselves, as we obsess over their unattainable body images and idyllic but unrealistic lifestyles, then perhaps we need to think about what we are getting from the relationship!

Trying to live up to these standards and constantly feeling inadequate takes its toll on our mental health, as it does on a lesser scale each time we log on and buy into the online lives apparently being lived by others in our immediate social circles also.

Going online to stoke our own anger

Another aspect of social media many people struggle with is the temptation to get drawn into debates on issues about which we have very intense feelings. We all have causes and issues that we care deeply about and we often use social media to find like-minded people to share our ideas with or to express support for causes we are passionate about. As the online community is open to a very diverse range of people, we will also inevitably find others that we may disagree with in very fundamental ways. With things being ever more polarised these days, dialogue and debate can get very heated on social media, and there can be a lot of comments and content that it will not serve any purpose for us to read. I'm not talking about ignoring people who are trying to provoke us - I'm talking about the potentially destructive habit of actively seeking out negative or provocative comments, and consuming large amounts of content that we know will only cause us anger and pain.

If we are reading to get a different perspective and the balanced views of others or hear some arguments that we may not have thought about, then wonderful. If we find we are reading purely to get ourselves riled up, then we should probably try and avoid it as much as possible. This is not good for our emotional health, and it can taint our view of the real world we actually live in where people are generally not shouting at us as we walk down the street.

Where from here?

Breaking the online habit can be a lot more difficult than you might think. The social media apps we use are designed to grab our attention, keep us engaged when we are there and call us back if we leave. If we have an objective look at the way we use social media and come to the conclusions that our constant engagement is having an effect on our daily lives and our relationships, then we need to try and break the cycle of interaction.

The following are some simple measures that make the process of disengagement easier.

→→ Turn off all social media notifications.

→ Don't install social media apps on your phone. In this way, if you want to access them, you have to browse for them each time.

→ Have a place at home where you leave the phone (preferably the hall) so that you will not be in constant contact with it.

→ Don't bring your phone to bed with you, so that checking it will no longer be the last thing you do at night and the first thing you do in the morning.

Ultimately, the best strategy of all is to ensure that we have something of greater value in our lives that will override and dispense with the constant need for escape. (We will be looking at this in more depth on page 268.)

Escape into pornography

In my early years in practice, I trained in a clinic that worked specifically with individuals who struggled with sex addiction. I counselled a lot of young men whose escape into pornography had become so problematic that they were seeking help to get back some sense of control over the situation. Many had had initial contact with porn in their early teens, with some discovering it as early as ten or eleven, and had used it as a coping mechanism long before they had developed any real sense of their own sexuality.

In this online age, engaging with porn seems to have become somewhat of a normalised activity in our society, as the internet has taken it off the top shelf and out of the seedy shops, to beam it into every home. Porn is now readily available, very affordable – often free – and, when it comes to escaping from unwanted thoughts and feelings, incredibly effective. This combination of instant accessibility and immediate effectiveness makes it highly addictive and the drug of choice for many young, especially male, individuals trying to get to grips with their lives and their emotions.

Like any means of escape, including the others we have discussed above, using porn becomes a real problem when we can no longer control when and for how long we engage with it. If the draw of pornography is keeping us from social interaction or means that we leave social situations early or we have tried to quit with little success, then it may be something other than a pastime.

The fact is that we usually don't know something is out of control until we have tried to control it and find we can't.

When the use of porn becomes a real problem, the length of time we spend on it can begin to have a negative impact in other parts of our lives. We may fancy a quick half-hour before bed but then find ourselves still engaged at 5.00 a.m. The issue here is that the goal of the exercise is not the orgasm, but staying in an intoxicated state and away from difficult emotions for as long as possible. In fact, the orgasm just signals the end of the escape, since when it is reached, we will be plunged straight back into reality, with all the fears, anxieties and difficult emotions that we were trying to get away from in the first place. So, the orgasm will be deliberately delayed and the porn session may go on for hours. However, by this point, our already intolerable feelings will only be compounded by the frustration we feel that our work alarm will be going off soon, our sense of helplessness at the fact that we can't control the acting out, as well as shame for engaging so uncontrollably in the first place.

This type of porn use is, by its very nature, secretive and done in isolation, and can leave us feeling frustrated, ashamed and possibly lonely, but it offers little risk and it can feel safe to the extent that it does not require leaving the house, spending a lot of money or getting out of our minds (with drink or drugs). Of course, it can also remove the need to contemplate the dreaded fear of intimacy or rejection that comes with attempted sexual interaction with a real human being. It is little wonder that online porn is so attractive. Like all drugs, however, if we continue to abuse it, the problem will progressively get worse, as our tolerance increases and we have to engage in it more and more to get an ever-decreasing reward.

Consequences

Like every escape mechanism that cuts off the emotions we cannot tolerate, the use of porn does not have the laser-like precision we would like - it doesn't just cut out anxiety and leave everything else intact. To use a harsh but fitting analogy, most weed killers will take out everything that is growing – and, in the same way, this level of engagement with pornography will leave all our emotions numbed, and has more significant potential for long-term effects than we imagine.

Work can be heavily affected, as we may call in sick a lot or regularly turn up utterly exhausted – and things can become especially problematic if we begin to use porn in the workplace to regulate anxiety. As the endless stream and variety of porn and the ease of access proves too much to resist, we are constantly being robbed of precious time to do the things we value or be with the people we love. If using porn is something we have done for a number of years, it will certainly have taken its toll on our self-worth, our ability to manage our emotions effectively, our relationships and our general wellbeing.

Stopping

With the overuse of porn can come an ambivalence towards the activity itself – a kind of love/hate relationship, where we want to give up, but the thought of not being able to engage is terrifying. In terms of taking the first steps to stop, if things are at a completely unmanageable level, quite drastic measures might be needed – such as not having wifi at home, downgrading smart phones or any other devices that can access the internet, and otherwise limiting our access no matter what the avenue. Cutting off access is a necessary immediate-term solution, because willpower alone will not beat this if it is already too far beyond our control.

The excessive use of porn also has complexities that

we would not find with substance abuse, and, in that sense, managing it can be more like trying to tackle difficulties with food. We come face-to-face with food every day, so if there is a problem there, it has to be managed, also with education around healthy eating and self-care. We don't necessarily come face-to-face with porn every day, but try to go for an hour in the modern world without seeing a sexualised image of one form of another – or a person we are attracted to for that matter. We also have a mind full of fantasies that we cannot easily get away from.

When it comes to stopping, awareness about the nature of the process itself can help. When we are engaging addictively with online porn or any other mood-altering stimulus, the process usually plays out something like this: preoccupation, then ritualisation and then acting out, followed by some level of emotional response, such as shame and guilt.

The preoccupation stage begins when an image or thought enters our head and we begin to obsess. This moves to ritualisation, as we think about how we can access the pornography and prepare the conditions to do so. This can include getting everything ready, turning off our phone, starting up our laptop, going to the comfortable spot we always go to, and so on. The ritual heightens the sense of anticipation and arousal. When we have acted out and the compulsion is over, we are left with the unmanaged emotions we needed to escape from in the first place, coupled with varying degrees of shame and guilt.

Trying to stop when we are too far into the process is extremely difficult. It's a bit like trying to stop a boulder from rolling down a hill. In the initial stages of small movement at the top of the hill, we have some chance, although slim, of stopping the boulder. When it gains momentum, however, we can forget about it. For someone who has a serious problem with porn, when the ritual has begun, there is no turning back. The ritual can also include measures like returning early from a night out, coming home from work and clearing your calendar so that the entire evening is free, and so on. This ritualisation is a key part of any addictive activity – a ritual for a smoker might be buying a cup of coffee or, at work, getting together with a fellow smoker to head downstairs from the office to the smoking area. It is all part of the experience and there are strong associations between the ritual and the event that heighten the sense of anticipation of the pleasure of the activity itself.

So, our only hope of breaking into this process is in the early stages of preoccupation. As with our negative worry thoughts, it might not feel like we have a choice about whether or not we engage, but, actually, we do. Similarly, when we are aware of what is happening, we can actively choose what to do next. The further we go into the process and the preoccupation, the harder it will be to make the right choice. So, as soon as we recognise we are getting drawn in, we have to step back and choose to do something different. Something of value to us. Something that will get us away from our phone or laptop for enough time for the moment to pass. By getting up and heading over to a friend's house, or phoning someone for a chat, we let our brain know we can take the emotions it wants us to escape and go about our day.

We need to expect this cycle and plan for it. If you are at home, alone on the couch, browsing through social media and the thought comes to mind, your ability to make the best choice will be diminished. Your brain will tell you it's all OK and that you should make the easiest choice. You need to give yourself the best chance possible to be able to step away. The best thing you can do is to be proactive and know these feelings will arise. You have to have plans in your life around being more engaged with people and be out of the house more, so that when you do get the first pangs of preoccupation, you are in a place where you may be able to let them pass. It's easy for your thoughts to go to porn if you are lonely or bored. Even if you are not out, if you have someone you trust who knows you are trying to kick this habit that you can phone in these times, it could be something that helps. It's often good to have someone outside ourselves to keep us accountable, but who we can trust not to shame us.

If you are at home, you need to stay away from the online world altogether. If you are looking through sports or news sites, it is the easiest thing to flick across to porn when the thought arises. To think you will have the willpower not to look is only fooling yourself.

Finally, if you have tried unsuccessfully to quit, you are no longer in control of when and for how long you engage and the knock-on effects on your life are many, it might be time to work with a professional who has experience and training in the area. What we have talked about here will not be enough to beat an intrusive, habitual problem and cannot hope to tackle the complexity of addiction. More specific and targeted work may be needed and having someone who is expert in the area would be of great benefit.

Motivation to stop

Whether we find ourselves caught up in the excessive use of social media or porn or any other maladaptive coping mechanism, it's important to be aware that stopping or breaking the habit will be a process rather than a quick fix. Just as there are no quick and easy ways to successfully address, once and for all, our anxieties or other feelings we do not want to feel, ending our overreliance on our chosen escape mechanism will involve a lot of patience and tolerance. If you visualise an iceberg floating in the ocean, the tip will represent the behaviour that we are looking to address. The bulk of the iceberg, however, is under water, and that is what is driving the behaviour.

We need to figure out if we are using the escape to deal with our anxiety or to numb other emotions. If we were to monitor ourselves for a week, would we find that we are more likely to reach for our escape activity when we are having anxious thoughts or bodily symptoms of anxiety or uncomfortable emotions? If we have been using escape mechanisms to regulate our emotions for a number of years and it has not worked, at what stage can we call it a failed experiment? It will never be a long-term solution to our anxiety. It just might be time to try something new. We do have to come to this realisation ourselves, however. We cannot get the motivation to recognise and address the problem from someone else – or from a book – but it might be worth thinking about.

Managing our anxiety

Managing our anxiety comes with the lessening of the overwhelming feeling of having no control over what is going on for us and what is making us feel this way. As we have seen throughout this book, when we start to unpack our issues and figure out both what we are dealing with and ways to address it, we can begin to tackle anxiety and learn to tolerate some of the feelings we once found unbearable. When we choose facing our fears over escape and avoidance, we find that we can cope, but we must always be aware that escape will very often seem like the easier and more appealing choice.

Very few of my clients looking to do work on their anxiety are over the moon about being in a counselling session. We'd all rather take an easier road, but we may likely discover that the easier road does not have the answers we need. We have to develop new, better coping mechanisms to replace the old ones, but the replacement phase may be long and painful, with ground gained and lost along the way. This will not have us suddenly shutting off all social media or immediately able to dispense with porn for good, but it will be an important step in the process of moving away from them.

Building relationships

If we find ourselves engaged in a very time-consuming, emotionally numbing activity that is taking us out of our reality, we might ask ourselves if we are ignoring the relationships in our lives or if we are lacking quality relationships of any note. Do we have friends? Are we close to them? What is our social structure like?

Having close relationships in which we can share what is going on for us and open up about difficulties we may be having is a great outlet. Talking is a powerful way to get our thoughts out of our heads so we can start to figure out what is happening for us. If we have someone who is willing to listen and give us space to express our thoughts and feelings, it can really help us work out some of the problems we may have. Often just saying something out loud to another non-judgemental person can bring an enormous amount of relief, without the need for any solution to be forthcoming. We do not always need to figure out what to do – sometimes we just need to express how we feel.

It may feel like a risk to share what we are feeling with others, so we often choose to say nothing and pretend everything is OK. We also may feel like we do not want to burden those close to us with our problems, but good friends are not there just for the good times, and if they sense there is something that we are dealing with alone, they will often want to be actively able to help.

However, we don't have to have friends with whom we are constantly sharing deep feelings. Often just being with other people, having fun or sharing interests can be beneficial for our mental health. Our friendships are very important and as we are highly social creatures, human contact can make such a difference to how we feel.

There can also be times when we feel there are very few people in our lives to whom we can turn, and friends are thin on the ground. Maybe we have not been good at maintaining friendships in the past or close friends have moved away or are not as accessible as they once were. Sometimes, we have to take a step out of our comfort zone and try to build a social network.

There are many ways to meet up with like-minded people these days, such as finding groups on the internet that meet close by, taking up a sport or other recreational interest or volunteering with a local charity. There are always ways to meet people, but we have to push ourselves and understand the importance of not isolating ourselves. Friendships, relationships and social contact with other people alone will not necessarily get us out of our maladaptive coping mechanisms, but they are a very important part of a bigger picture.

Replacing escape with something you value

Access to social media or porn is so prevalent these days that, over time, we need to be sure to replace our need to escape with something meaningful – preferably lots of meaningful things. Sometimes, boredom and pure force of habit can play a part in our repeated use of maladaptive coping mechanisms.

We've talked about friendships and these would be a good start. Work that challenges us would also help, rather than doing a job we dislike or even hate just to survive. In Chapters 7 and 8 (Anxiety in the Workplace – Parts One and Two), we looked at coming out of our comfort zones, facing some fears and pushing ourselves to put ourselves forward. It is worth taking the time to think about what we could achieve, and how much more fulfilled we would feel, if we were able to adopt some of these approaches in our own lives.

Something outside of work that we are engaged in would also be very beneficial to our general well-being. Something we enjoy and which is productive – like a course, further learning or a hobby of some sort. Exercise is a great one for both our physical and mental health. All of this will take time and energy away from our indulging in our unhealthier escape activities but, if our primary goal is finding more meaning in our lives and doing things we value, then these habits will begin to lose their power over us.

A good question to ask ourselves is this: What are the things and activities I value and enjoy in my life so much that, when I am engaged in them, I don't feel the need to escape into fantasy? We need to identify these things and do more of them, and also find more activities and interests that give us this feeling. As well as thinking about what escape is taking from our lives, we can also look at what our lives would be like if we got this time back by focusing on things that bring us a sense of meaning and fulfilment.

Chapter 14
And Finally . . .

I remember what my brain said to me immediately after I was asked by my publisher if I had an idea for a book . . . 'Well, yes, you do - but you don't have an idea for a second book.'

What?

'What if the first one goes OK, and they ask you to write a second one? What then?'

Oh . . .

That's where my brain instantly went to. Not 'What a great opportunity! or 'Isn't this fantastic?' No - instant danger.

This is what my brain does, what it always has done - and possibly always will do. Especially when faced with change, uncertainty and challenge. I'll overestimate the potential threat and underestimate my own ability to cope. As I said at the very beginning of this book, as far as is humanly possible, I have now made my peace with the way my brain works. It usually doesn't get the better of me but, sometimes, it still does.

Maybe in this instance, it was the newness or uniqueness of the situation, but I entertained these negative thoughts about the prospect of writing a book for many hours before realising what was happening. It initially felt important for me to listen to the thoughts because the feelings they brought up were so strong and so familiar. I immediately started arguing with my brain, trying to rationalise my thinking, but these thoughts could not be negotiated with.

Something large and uncertain had entered my world, and my brain had gone into full-blown self-protection mode. When I could see what was going on, I was fairly quickly able to quieten my mind. 'OK, Brain, I hear you, but we'll let Future Stew deal with it. I've got a client coming soon, so let's focus on that for now. Come on, let's go!'

learning to see things differently

I discovered something important about my approach to the task of putting together this book when I was about halfway through writing it – and the realisation certainly made writing the second half a lot more comfortable.

As a way of ensuring that I would be able to finish the text before the deadline, I had set myself a target number of words to be written every week, which I did not let myself miss. On Sunday nights, I would creep over my target line, meaning that on Monday mornings, the counter was set to zero again. It had a relentless element to it, but I knew that, if I did not work like this, I would start getting anxious and end up getting in my own way, and would never be able to finish the book.

Each week, I would have days when I would be able to write freely and other days on which the words were so slow to come. During these less productive days – which, in retrospect, I have now labelled my 'thinking days' – my brain kicked in with the usual anxious thoughts: 'You're never going to be able to do this. I can't believe you even thought this was possible to begin with. Who do you think you are kidding? You're going to have to go back to the publisher and tell them you've made an awful mistake.'

At the end of such days, I'd go home and my family would get a quieter, more distracted, less present version of me. My sleep would not be as good and, the next day, I would be reluctant to start on productive work, until each time I proved to myself that, yes, indeed, I could actually put a few words together and that the previous day had been just a blip. I had made these 'thinking days' mean something they didn't – I'd made them mean that I was not able to hit my targets and from that, my wonderful mind had extrapolated that I couldn't write a book at all and that I was a failure and was bound to fail at this task too. (Thanks, Brain!).

At a certain point, however, I decided that it was the slow days that actually made the fast days possible. It was just a simple change in the way I allowed myself to see things, but the result was that my brain no longer saw those days as a threat, and the negative thoughts began to quieten. It didn't make the less productive days any easier to get through in one sense, but I found I wasn't left with the same unsatisfied feeling in the pit of my stomach as I had been. My brain was no longer telling me that I was up against it, making the rest of the week so much harder for me. I was able to see this as part of the bigger process, and that the difficult days with few words were what enabled the times when the words flowed, the times that made me feel both good about myself and more confident that I could actually complete the project.

When I was struggling with the amount I was writing and feeling down about it, I used some of the other strategies outlined in previous chapters, and they really worked. I broadened the timeline and looked at my output for that week, and not that particular day or hour. Again, I realised that it was perfectly fine to be writing next to nothing on some days, when overall the week was going well.

When I was feeling overwhelmed about the sheer volume of work I had ahead of me, I simply contracted the timeline right down, and focused on the work I had to do that day. I also decided not to get annoyed with myself when my thoughts inevitably ran ahead into worries about the future. As soon as I caught them, I brought them back into the present, so I could bring my full attention to the task immediately in front of me. Each time my thoughts would fly off, I brought them back again, knowing that if I blew up at myself, I would be in no state to get anything done.

I guess the moral of this tale is that managing worry and anxiety is, in a lot of ways, like writing this book. It's a constant - we get to Sunday, having worked all week to keep things under control, and then Monday comes around and we have to start all over again! If we begin asking why we have to keep dealing with such worrisome thoughts and thinking how unfair life is for those of us who suffer from anxiety, then things get infinitely harder. If, however, we can view the days when we are anxious as opportunities to get better at tackling our difficulties and managing our thoughts, then we are better placed to succeed in the long run.

These days and this work are what will enable us to enjoy the better days, when things are easier. And things do get easier, just as the better days will begin to come around more often.

'But what if it gets easier for a little while and then it gets bad again?'

I hear you, Brain - you'll never quit. Come on, Future Stew will handle it - right now, we have other things to do!'

Further Reading list

Social Anxiety

Overcoming Social Anxiety and Shyness: A self-help guide to using cognitive behavioural techniques by Gillian Butler (Robinson, 1999)

'A Cognitive Perspective on Social Phobia', David M Clark: Chapter 18, *International Handbook of Social Anxiety: Concepts, Research and Interventions relating to the Self and Shyness*, ed./W Crozier; LE Alden (John Wiley, New York, 2001), pp. 405. The text of the chapter can be downloaded from the King's College London Research Portal, as follows:

https://kclpure.kcl.ac.uk/portal/en/publications/a-cognitive-perspective-on-social-phobia(c8655ab4-d216-4a28-ada4-e658a53ffde7)/export.html

Worry

Overcoming Worry and Generalised Anxiety Disorder – A Self-Help Guide using Cognitive Behavioural Techniques, Kevin Meares and Mark Freeston (Robinson, 2008; 2015)

The Worry Cure – Seven Steps to Stop Worry from Stopping You, Dr Robert L Leahy (Random House, 2006)

Relationships

The 5 Love Languages: The Secret to Love that Lasts, Gary Chapman (Moody Press, 2015)

Sex addiction

Facing the Shadow: Starting Sexual and Relationship Recovery, Patrick Carnes (Gentle Path Press, 2015)

Mindfulness

Mindfulness: A Practical Guide to Finding Peace in a Frantic World, Mark Williams and Danny Penman, (Piatkus, 2011)

General Personal Growth

Mastery: The Keys to Success and Long-term Fulfilment, George Leonard (Plume (Penguin), 1992)

Mind Over Mood: Change How You Feel by Changing the Way You Think, Dennis Greenberger and Christine A Padesky (Guilford Press, Second Edition, 1995)

Reinventing your life: The Breakthrough Program to End Negative Behaviour and Feel Great Again, Jeffrey E Young and Janet S Klosko (Plume (Penguin), 1993)

The Happiness Trap: Stop Struggling, Start Living (Based on ACT: A revolutionary mindfulness-based programme for overcoming stress, anxiety and depression), Russ Harris (Robinson, 2008)

Acknowledgements

There are many people who have been instrumental in getting this book out of my head and onto paper. I would like to start by thanking Ciara Doorley and Joanna Smyth of Hachette Books Ireland, for contacting me out of the blue and asking if I had thought about a potential book. Then for walking me through the process of writing and always being there to answer my many questions. To my editor, Susan Feldstein of The Feldstein Agency, a special thank you for giving me invaluable feedback and for all the work she put in getting the original manuscript to the book it is now.

To Oonagh, my wonderful wife, thanks for being my sounding board and my first editor, and especially for shouldering the burden of a young family while I was off writing the book. Your love and support make the difficult things in my life manageable and the hard times tolerable. For giving me the ability to put everything into perspective, I also owe my two boys, Douglas and Ross, a huge thank you.

I am so grateful to all my clients from whom I have learned so much about my own journey and theirs. My parents, my sister, my friends, my therapists and supervisors, my managers, my mentors, all added to my growth and learning. To all, my gratitude.